**New Directions for
Student Leadership**

Susan R. Komives
EDITOR-IN-CHIEF

Kathy L. Guthrie
ASSOCIATE EDITOR

D1446304

Engaging Youth in Leadership for Social and Political Change

Michael P. Evans

Kathleen Knight Abowitz

EDITORS

Number 148 • Winter 2015
Jossey-Bass
San Francisco

ENGAGING YOUTH IN LEADERSHIP FOR SOCIAL AND POLITICAL CHANGE
Michael P. Evans, Kathleen Knight Abowitz (eds.)
New Directions for Student Leadership, No. 148, Winter 2015

Susan R. Komives, Editor-in-Chief
Kathy L. Guthrie, Associate Editor

Microfilm copies of issues and articles are available in 16mm and 35mm, as well as microfiche in 105mm, through University Microfilms Inc., 300 North Zeeb Road, Ann Arbor, MI 48106-1346.

New Directions for Student Leadership is indexed in Academic Search Alumni Edition (EBSCO Publishing), Education Index/Abstracts (EBSCO Publishing), ERA: Educational Research Abstracts Online (T&F), ERIC: Educational Resources Information Center (CSC), MLA International Bibliography (MLA).

NEW DIRECTIONS FOR STUDENT LEADERSHIP (ISSN 2373-3349, electronic ISSN 2373-3357) is part of the Jossey-Bass Higher and Adult Education Series and is published quarterly by Wiley Subscription Services, Inc., A Wiley Company, at Jossey-Bass, One Montgomery Street, Suite 1200, San Francisco, CA 94104-4594. POSTMASTER: Send all address changes to New Directions for Student Leadership, Jossey-Bass, One Montgomery Street, Suite 1200, San Francisco, CA 94104-4594.

SUBSCRIPTIONS for print only: $89.00 for individuals in the U.S./Canada/Mexico; $113.00 international. For institutions, agencies, and libraries, $342.00 U.S.; $382.00 Canada/Mexico; $416.00 international. Electronic only: $89.00 for individuals all regions; $342.00 for institutions all regions. Print and electronic: $98.00 for individuals in the U.S., Canada, and Mexico; $122.00 for individuals for the rest of the world; $411.00 for institutions in the U.S.; $451.00 for institutions in Canada and Mexico; $485.00 for institutions for the rest of the world. Prices subject to change. Refer to the order form that appears at the back of most volumes of this journal.

EDITORIAL CORRESPONDENCE should be sent to the Associate Editor, Kathy L. Guthrie, at kguthrie@fsu.edu.

Cover design: Wiley
Cover Images: © Lava 4 images | Shutterstock

www.josseybass.com

CONTENTS

EDITORS' NOTES

Youth are learning lessons in leadership and democratic life every day. These lessons occur in traditional brick-and-mortar classrooms when a 10th-grade U.S. Government class watches a documentary about Franklin Delano Roosevelt and the New Deal. Down the hall a ninth-grade English class is preparing to take a multiple-choice quiz on the first three chapters of *The Autobiography of Malcolm X*. Lessons in democratic engagement take place when a student in California is asked to turn his graphic tee inside out because it violates the school dress code or when a group of students in Detroit are suspended for staging a walkout to protest a school closure. These lessons take place as youth use social media to crowdsource funding for student organizations or when they share clips of an interview with former Arkansas governor Mike Huckabee from an episode of *The Daily Show with Jon Stewart*. These lessons occur as youth witness their family and neighbors take to the streets to participate in the Occupy Movement or Black Lives Matter.

Examples of leadership and democratic life are all around us. Elliot Eisner (1979) discussed how educational institutions teach with the use of a combination of three curricula: explicit, implicit, and null. The explicit curriculum refers to the curriculum of public record in course catalogs. Implicit curriculum includes that values and beliefs that are informally conveyed through school or college culture. The null curriculum is defined as what schools or colleges do not teach. Although Eisner's framework was focused on the work of schools, it can also help us consider how youth absorb leadership lessons through their lived experience.

The Eisner framework (1979) is useful for hypothesizing about what understandings and knowledge youth are working from as they engage in public life. Young adults in high school and postsecondary settings have, through their formal educational experiences, been exposed to narrow iterations of civic knowledge through the explicit, taught curriculum in social studies or political science courses. Peter Levine (2011), Director of the Center for Information and Research on Civic Learning and Engagement, analyzes the National Assessment of Educational Progress test results and argues that the U.S. scores indicate students learn skills in constitutional and legal analysis better than content knowledge of political life and processes. Explicit civics curriculum may not be adequately teaching politics and political change processes.

NEW DIRECTIONS FOR STUDENT LEADERSHIP, no. 148, Winter 2015 © 2015 Wiley Periodicals, Inc., A Wiley Company
Published online in Wiley Online Library (wileyonlinelibrary.com) • DOI: 10.1002/yd.20148

What other types of knowledge are left out of the explicit curriculum? The null curriculum of civic leadership, or those bodies of knowledge or practice that we do not teach, is often skills and knowledge related to everyday politics, civic agency, and shared leadership for political and social change. This distinction between explicit and the null curriculum of leadership for democratic change highlights how conventional understandings of democracy, citizenship, and leadership education are often counter to, or at least incomplete, in preparing youth to make change in their society.

In addition to the explicit, taught curriculum of civics and government and the null curriculum consisting of everyday political agency, are the implicit lessons we receive about leadership and democracy in our culture. Students spend most of their school years learning to submit quietly to the rules of adult authorities, and social discourses on leadership tend to valorize the trope of the charismatic leader. Democratic politics, as portrayed by national media outlets, seems largely a dysfunctional game that benefits the most powerful. Confidence in government as expressed in national polls is at historic lows (Pew Research Center, 2011).

The purpose of this issue is to consider alternative ways of thinking about youth leadership education. The authors in this issue reveal the power of educators and youth who see possibilities beyond those taught through most explicit and implicit curricula in our schools or media networks. Rather than simply reproduce old meanings of leadership from past generations, these authors address how institutions and individuals can work with youth to enable the capacity to critique, shape, and enact new meanings of leadership in a democratic society.

Youth leadership initiatives can help young people engage in democratic life, participatory governance, and organizing for social and political change. Spanning in and beyond the secondary and postsecondary landscapes, youth leadership programs, curricula, and opportunities can develop in community centers, schools, online, or on the streets, to meet critical challenges in communities. Although many youth leadership programs have carefully avoided political topics or skill-building because they are insufficiently neutral for ideologically diverse student groups or potentially controversial, new political engagement opportunities are placing leadership learning in the context of civic life, where democratic politics often feature challenging community issues and conflicts. Leadership education for coming generations of citizens is taking on new forms and meanings, as educators, organizers, and youth themselves seek to build the social intelligence and competence needed to educate citizen–leaders. These new forms often cross borders—identities, institutions, regions, and nation-states. This volume explores those new meanings through examining the theories and practices constituting the emerging ground of public leadership.

When we began to prepare this issue, it was our intention to create a publication that would be helpful for individuals working with youth and college students in public leadership with an eye toward emergent issues to be discussed in the national elections in 2016. We still believe that this issue is helpful in this regard, but we are now more cognizant of the contextualized nature of public leadership work.

During the months leading up to publication, the United States was embroiled in debates regarding the use of fatal force by police. As a result, several chapters use Black Lives Matter as a foundation for their work. In addition, there is a noteworthy lack of research here related to more traditional political parties or electoral politics as venues for leadership and social change; this may reflect a loss of confidence in these institutions by U.S. citizens, and by Millennials and Generation X groups more acutely. Simply put, leadership education for political and social change is necessarily situated in current events and immediate contexts in a way that traditional leadership education is not.

A curriculum for leadership education oriented toward political and social change must continue to evolve in response to the lived experience of youth, particularly those who live in the most difficult contexts. We have attempted to capture the complexity of these efforts by including chapters that span secondary and higher education programs, local and international contexts, school-based and out-of-school-time initiatives, and a broad diversity of youth.

Michael P. Evans
Kathleen Knight Abowitz
Editors

References

Eisner, E. (1979). *The educational imagination* (Vol. 103). New York, NY: Macmillan.

Levine, P. (2011, May 4). Some surprising results from the 2010 NAEP Civics assessment. *CIRCLE Blog*. Retrieved from http://www.civicyouth.org/some-surprising-results-from-the-2010-naep-civics-assessment/

Pew Research Center. (2014, November 13). Public trust in government: 1958–2014. Retrieved from http://www.people-press.org/2014/11/13/public-trust-in-government/

MICHAEL P. EVANS *is associate professor of family, school and community connections at Miami University. He holds a joint appointment in teacher education, educational leadership, and family studies and social work. Dr. Evans also coordinates an undergraduate minor in community-based leadership. His primary research interest is community-based approaches to educational change with an emphasis on grassroots organizing.*

KATHLEEN KNIGHT ABOWITZ *is professor and chair of the Department of Educational Leadership at Miami University. She teaches philosophy of education and community leadership courses in the department, and helped launch Miami University's community-based leadership minor program. Her scholarship focuses on conceptions of the democracy, the public, democratic education, and leadership for public educational institutions (K–16).*

NEW DIRECTIONS FOR STUDENT LEADERSHIP • DOI: 10.1002/yd

This chapter addresses the overemphasis on individual-leader development in leadership education, offering insights and pragmatic approaches for advancing collective leadership focused on social and political change.

Beyond Individual Leader Development: Cultivating Collective Capacities

John P. Dugan, Natasha T. Turman, Mark A. Torrez

Paolo Freire's (2000) quote "The revolution is made neither by the leaders for the people, nor by the people for the leaders, but by both acting together in unshakable solidarity" beautifully illustrates the ways in which the struggle for political and social change reflects a shared humanity that is inextricably intertwined (p. 129). It is a reminder of the critical need for leadership grounded in community, focused on the cultivation of collective capacities, and characterized by an unwavering emphasis on social justice. Indeed, leadership scholarship increasingly reflects these values, espousing social change as a primary goal (Dugan & Velázquez, 2015; Komives, Wagner, & Associates, 2009; Preskill & Brookfield, 2009). Yet the actual educational practice of leadership development has not kept pace. Scholars have begun to question the degree to which leadership education continues to allow leader development (i.e., preparation of individuals to engage successfully in leader roles and processes) to trump leadership development (i.e., the preparation of groups and/or collectives to engage successfully in leadership processes). This is further complicated by the perpetuation of skill-based learning characterized by command-and-control achievement orientations and the replication of singular narratives, or the telling of one narrative as a standard for a given experience, that are both exclusionary and fail to capture community-based approaches (Dugan & Velázquez, 2015; Uhl-Bien & Ospina, 2012).

The purpose of this chapter is to address the gap between espoused values and actual practice by decentering individual-leader development and focusing on pragmatic ways in which leadership education can better cultivate the collective capacities necessary to advance social and political

NEW DIRECTIONS FOR STUDENT LEADERSHIP, no. 148, Winter 2015 © 2015 Wiley Periodicals, Inc., A Wiley Company
Published online in Wiley Online Library (wileyonlinelibrary.com) • DOI: 10.1002/yd.20149

5

change. The chapter starts by examining the concepts of individual-leader development, offering insights and illustrations of how deeply these perspectives are woven into our consciousness, as well as the very leadership models crafted to address leadership for social and political change. Close examination of these themes is essential for leadership educators' professional development. We then offer two pragmatic ways in which educators can alter leadership interventions to address these concerns.

The Vexing Nature of Leader Versus Leadership Development

Day, Harrison, and Halpin (2009) articulated the primacy of leader development in the process of leadership development, suggesting that the ability to serve effectively as a leader precedes capacities for group-leadership effectiveness. They ground this claim in substantial research. Yet, in a recent book chapter on relational leadership approaches, Day and Drath (2012) debated what are often-uncontested assumptions. Drath, as cited in Day and Drath (2012), challenged that "there are collectives in which leader development is not needed to develop leadership, simply because leadership happens without leaders" (p. 237). Ultimately, leader and leadership development are both of value, but their relative importance may be contingent on any number of factors, ranging from cultural to organizational contexts. More concerning may be the fact that if leadership education rarely gets to the complex processes of leadership development, then we may be hindering the readiness of both individuals and collectives to address social and political change.

The tension between leader and leadership development is perhaps most evident in leadership theory, which disproportionately focuses on preparation for formal leader roles. More recently, scholars have introduced models with alternative approaches. This includes the social change model of leadership development (Higher Education Research Institute [HERI], 1996), which is routinely cited as among the most common models applied in college youth leadership education (Kezar, Carducci, & Contreras-McGavin, 2006; Owen, 2012). The social change model approaches leadership as a "purposeful, collaborative, values-based process that results in positive social change" (Komives et al., 2009, p. xii). Key tenets of the model include the acknowledgment that leadership happens both in and outside of formal positions and is inherently collaborative in nature. Moreover, the model describes the essential function of leadership as a vehicle for social responsibility and justice.

Figure 1.1 provides a visual representation of the model, which identifies seven key values (consciousness of self, congruence, commitment, collaboration, common purpose, controversy with civility, citizenship) that undergird socially responsible leadership (HERI, 1996; Komives et al., 2009). These values cluster across three domains (the individual, the group, the societal); reflect capacities; and are composed of requisite knowledge, skills,

Figure 1.1.   The Social Change Model of Leadership Development

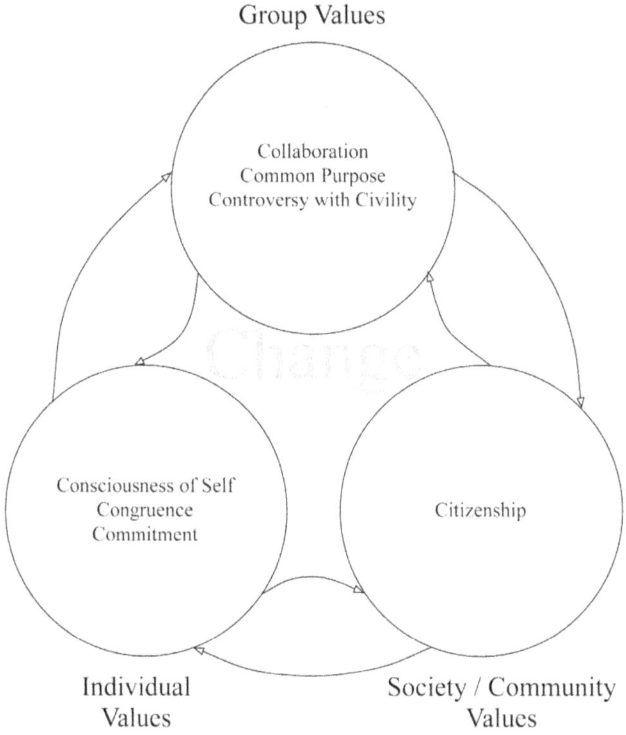

Group Values

Individual
Values

Society / Community
Values

Adapted from Higher Education Research Institute (1996). Copyright © 1996, National Clear-inghouse for Leadership Programs. Reprinted with permission of the National Clearinghouse for Leadership Programs.

and attitudes. Collectively, they contribute to the overarching capacity to engage effectively in the work of social change. The model is designed from both a process perspective (i.e., what does it look like to engage in leadership?) and a developmental perspective (i.e., what are the individual and collective capacities that enhance the ability to engage in leadership?).

Interestingly, educational efforts that employ the social change model almost uniformly take the developmental perspective and focus on individual outcome achievement. The work of the model becomes how best to build individuals' abilities in the seven values and across the three domains, thus increasing their overall capacity for socially responsible leadership. Much less common is a framing of the social change model in which the group builds collective capacities across the values. This is likely indicative of the overreliance on leader development in leadership education. More problematically, the role of community is often framed as one to be acted upon as opposed to learned from and engaged with in partnership. Despite best intentions, an overemphasis on individual development neglects the social change model's process dimensions. To adjust for this requires insight into why educators may consciously and unconsciously avoid collective approaches. In the sections that follow we discuss three factors that potentially explain this avoidance.

The Myth of the Meritocracy. American dream ideology (Truslow Adams, 1931) serves as a powerful primer of hyperindividualism and cultural indoctrination. The myth of a meritocracy continues to influence cultural messaging and socialization processes across race, gender, nationality, and social class, sending powerful narratives that link individual achievement to success (Hochschild, 1995). The lived experiences of millions of people with nondominant group memberships serve as evidence that the American meritocracy is more pipe dream than reality. Consequently, many neighborhoods operate less like communities and more like random groupings of geographically proximal individuals competing for resources, with little motivation to engage in collective leadership. As a result, individuals are rarely prepared to collaborate and learn across differences; recognize their unique location within social systems; or enact the cultural, moral, and organizational flexibility essential to movements for social and political change. In leadership education this may also reinforce the perceived need for individual leader development over collective leadership development in the design and delivery of programs contributing to a self-replicating system that continuously reinforces individualism.

Fatalism. Along with a lack of investment in cultivating collective leadership capacity, communities are also challenged by a culture of fatalism. Defined by Freire (2000), fatalism is the belief that the world into which one is born is static and predetermined. This notion was largely informed by Freire's interviews with peasants who felt powerless to revolt against the masters who ruled them. As leadership educators, our responsibility is to stand in direct opposition to this ideology, to teach others that they can change the world that they were born into for the better. Yet, many youth are engrained with fatalistic attitudes from an early age directly related to unnamed power structures. As children, the most powerful question asked may be "Why?" And as adults, the most sabotaging responses may be "Because it just is," "Because I said so," or more specifically, "Because I am the authority and I said so." At home and throughout educational systems, youth are implicitly and explicitly socialized to defer in the presence of perceived power and authority. In leadership education we may both reproduce power dynamics and contribute to fatalism by not addressing these factors directly. To what degree do leadership interventions assist individuals and groups in naming and understanding complex power and authority relationships in their lives?

Individualism and the Dismissal of Activism. The cultivation of fierce individualism contributes to social conditioning that erodes the value of and obscures collective leadership movements. Youth are inculcated with individualistic leadership ideology often creatively camouflaged by (a) superhero fantasies, (b) overemphasis on untouchable and fictitiously per-fected role models like Abraham Lincoln and Martin Luther King, Jr., and (c) a compulsive dependency on individual achievement as the metric of success. Furthermore, collective movements are often labeled not as leader-ship, but activism, and are derided as unsustainable. This messaging posi-tions collective movements as both episodic and undesirable. It is important to acknowledge that there are communities with significantly stronger in-vestments in communal messaging around social responsibility. However, even within these more collectivist communities, "implicit and explicit sup-port of existing systems based in part on the beliefs, ideas, and worldviews [individuals] inherited," often enables ruling dominant ideologies to per-meate community values (Gross, 2011, p. 52). As a consequence, individu-als may become pulled toward individualistic rhetoric that both privileges and encourages the pursuit of traditional forms of leadership through dom-inant cultural practices like competition. This is readily apparent in leader-ship education curricula through the pervasive usage of heroic leaders and extraordinary cases, and the absence of learning goals related to strategic organizing and community-based change.

Reconstructing Collective Leadership for Social and Political Change

We propose that the pervasive culture of individualism and growing fatalism within Western societies has resulted in a widespread delimitation of agency and is devastating community leadership and well-being. We define *agency* as the capacity to act within a social system and as a primary mechanism as-sociated with leadership for social and political change. Thus, a shift to lead-ership development must divest in hyperindividualism and cultivate collec-tive agency. Kumashiro (2002) reminds us that educational institutions and pedagogy do not operate apart from social structures and dominant ideolo-gies; rather, they can serve as "apparatuses that transmit ruling ideologies, maintain hegemony, and reproduce existing social order" (p. 45). We see this play out directly in leadership education that overemphasizes leader development. Kumashiro (2002) advocated for a critically reconstructed form of education in which identity, power, and privilege serve as primary lenses for learning. Leveraging this argument, we offer two pragmatic ways in which leadership educators can alter interventions by raising power con-sciousness and centering the work of collective movements. Along with this we offer reconstructed approaches to working with the social change model that better align with leadership development focused on social and politi-cal change.

   Raising Power Consciousness.   The interrelated processes of devel-oping power consciousness and agency are aptly captured by Freire (1995) as "learning 'to perceive social, political, and economic contradictions,' and to take action against the oppressive elements of reality" (as cited in

Kumashiro, 2002, p. 46). Developing power consciousness involves a multifaceted transformation of perception that requires individuals to recognize their own social identities and the ways in which they have been ascribed certain power or privileges, and/or oppressed, within dominant social structures. Beyond the recognition of historical privileges and oppression, power consciousness also acknowledges the ways in which one actively seeks and wields power—how one consents to, perpetuates, or resists dominant systems. It is through this dual process of recognizing how one is both a subject to and object of power that agency is cultivated.

However, raising power consciousness does not just occur through individual learning. A reconstruction focused on leadership development requires that groups engage in the process of understanding their collective power as well as the ways in which power flows socially and organizationally. This includes closely examining dominant understandings of social capital (i.e., connections within and between personal networks) as a form of individual power. Yosso's (2005) work on community cultural wealth, defined as "an array of knowledge, skills, abilities, and contacts possessed and utilized by communities of color to survive and resist macro and microforms of oppression" (p. 77), substantiated the usefulness of fostering collectivism by calling attention to the ways in which community belonging bolsters multiple forms of power. This shifts understandings of and learning around power, emphasizing group approaches to navigating power dynamics, ultimately cultivating greater agency and resilience.

Pragmatic approaches to raising power consciousness in leadership development start with what Liu (2013) refers to as "power literacy." This involves naming power dynamics explicitly rather than allowing them to operate in the background. It also involves the introduction of power literacy to youth at much younger ages so that they can begin to examine their relationships with power and authority in social interactions. An excellent approach to this involves using Liu's TEDTalk in which he discusses mapping as a key strategy for developing skills associated with recognizing and navigating power. He outlines eight essential prompts on power for critical self-reflection and educational dialogue:

1. What is power?
2. Who has it?
3. How does it operate?
4. How does it flow?
5. What part of it is visible?
6. What part of it is not?
7. Why do some people have it?
8. Why is that compounded?

Although the initial stages of developing power consciousness or literacy entail largely personal reflections about one's social location, Liu's

(2013) eight prompts offer a framework for power mapping as a tool for leadership development. Within any specific context or situation, power can be defined, identified, described, and traced through mapping. Groups benefit when leadership education pushes them to consider the flow of power as it plays out in their efforts toward social and political change. This can be done by first engaging with the prompt questions and then creating visual representations that capture power dynamics. For communities engaging in social change efforts, a power map of an organization or of the greater community can be instrumental in instilling individual and collective agency through learning the systematic practices and flow of power.

Raising power consciousness offers a tool to deconstruct limitations associated with the social change model of leadership development. Despite a clear focus on social justice and recognition of community and societal systems, writing on the social change model often fails to address the reality of systematic power and authority dynamics inherent to all social change processes explicitly. Educators working with the model are encouraged to engage individuals and collectives in the process of self-exploration associated with raising power consciousness. Liu's (2013) power mapping prompts can be employed to examine broadly the history and systematic structures of power within a given society. More importantly, educators can engage youth in more advanced leadership learning by contextualizing the prompts in the specific community, organization, and/or situation in which they are engaged in social and political change. Questions like "what is power?" "who has it?" and "how does it flow?" help groups to describe and trace power dynamics as well as translate these insights into informed decision making and greater agency. The social change model benefits when it is described as unfolding within multiple, overlapping systems of power. Additionally, educators should consider adding a value to the model focusing on individual and group capacity for power literacy.

Centering Collective Movements.   Collective leadership is at the heart of leadership development, as it creates contexts characterized by truly shared learning, disruption of leader/follower binaries, and fluidity of leader roles. This contributes to a leadership dynamic in which individual capacities are transformed into collective capacities greater than the sum of their parts. It also centers critical group capacities related to social perspective-taking (the ability to understand another person or group's point of view as well as infer their thoughts and feelings), establishes interest convergence (perception of mutual benefit from a particular issue typically on the part of a dominant group), and promotes solidarity (social ties that bind groups around common sympathies, beliefs, and interests; for example, advocating support of a community ballot initiative).

Preskill and Brookfield (2009) articulate the daunting barriers that contribute to resistance and, ultimately, serve to block collective approaches:

Ego, the personal difficulty of learning to compromise, traditional leadership models, lack of faith in the ability of people to accomplish great things together, organizational reward systems that encourage individual competition and discourage collaboration, the wider ideological privileging of individuality, the power of myths and mores of the self-made man and pioneer woman, capitalism's emphasis on competition as a natural way of life, bureaucracy's attempt to sift and order people in terms of their specific accomplishments, levels, personality types, leadership styles, and so on—all of these things stand in the way of collective leadership making a difference. (p. 91)

And yet, collective leadership does make a difference. History is replete with examples of communities working together to create social and political change. The year 2014 embodied collective leadership with communities across the nation and internationally, standing in solidarity as their interests converged to combat oppressive rules, policies, and behaviors. College campuses, local communities, student groups, and collectives on social media platforms engaged in social perspective-taking, forging bonds and rallying together to proclaim, "Pro-democratic elections in Hong Kong," "Black lives matter," "Bring back our girls," "I can't breathe," "Hands up, don't shoot," "$15 hourly wages," and "SOS for Mexico." Although each of these movements varied in purpose, some serving as a catalyst for others, they all personified, as noted in the work of Heifetz and Linsky (2002), an "exercise of leadership that moved beyond the day-to-day stakes" (p. 209) to ones that valued community, interconnection, engagement, and love (Boggs & Kurashige, 2012). Thus, we share the list of barriers to collective leadership not to contribute to fatalism, but to highlight how despite such significant odds, collective leadership continues to work. Understanding the barriers also provides specific points of entry from which educators can design leadership development interventions that move beyond day-to-day stakes and focus on the work of social and political change. Each form of resistance is an opportunity to create learning experiences that deconstruct commonly held beliefs. (See Chapter 3, "Radically healing black lives: A love note to justice," for a close analysis of "Black lives matter" as a collective leadership movement.)

Advancing collective leadership necessitates pragmatic approaches that center collective movements within leadership development curricula. First, educators must help youth clearly distinguish leader and leadership development and understand the roles of each in contributing to social and political change. Second, curricula must be stripped away of the overreliance on overly theoretical or heroic leader figures used to illustrate and teach leadership development. This means infusing collective movements as primary examples throughout the curriculum, as well as highlighting the importance of coalition building between/among collectives, which can be incredibly difficult, as even those advocating collective leadership often slip into the use of individuals as examples. Feminist scholar and activist

Grace Lee Boggs offers a brilliant recasting of movement leaders as movement architects who serve as catalysts for the critical connections necessary for systemic change (Boggs & Kurashige, 2012). Movement architects "transform and empower participants," they acknowledge the humanity in those around them, and they aspire to create dynamic transformation that impacts both self and society (Boggs & Kurashige, 2012, p. 99). Therefore, educational interventions should similarly leverage community, relationships, and everyday lived experiences as the primary mechanisms of collective leadership to avoid dehumanizing this work through the over use of theory. This also means avoiding the perpetuation of heroic myths that undermine collective movements and centering the community and social system first. For example, leadership curricula should study the Civil Rights Movement rather than just Martin Luther King, Jr. This shift divests from the hyperindividualism of the American dream meritocracy pipe dream to allow for the many voices of the movement to surface, positioning King as a key movement architect engaged in collective leadership.

One way to approach the centering of collective movements is through the use of contemporary examples for which history has yet to ascribe individual heroes. By exposing students to real-world movements, they gain a window into collective leadership for social and political change. The award-winning documentary *The Square*, directed by Jehane Noujaim (2013), follows multiple movement architects and participants alike as it tracks multiple stages of the Egyptian Revolution. The film offers deep insights into how those involved with the revolution navigated shared decision making, struggled to build and maintain solidarity, nurtured interest convergence, and evolved their abilities to engage in social perspective-taking, all while navigating multiple, complex social power structures. It is an ideal movie to show students at the start of leadership development efforts, as it disrupts both heroic myths and utopian views of how social and political changes are achieved. It also establishes a common frame of reference for shared learning.

The centering of collective movements also presents an opportunity for reconstructing how educators employ the social change model. Recall that the model offers both a developmental perspective related to building capacity and a process perspective. The latter is often neglected. The analysis of collective movements offers a means to stay focused on how the process of collective leadership unfolds. With the social change model used as a framework, students can examine the degree to which particular values are at play, and how their presence and/or absence influences events, relationships, and outcomes. This also affords an opportunity for students to reconstruct the social change model itself, with the collective movement used as validation for the addition, alteration, or adaptation of elements. The impact of this has significant potential to increase agency and support students' perceptions of their own authoritative voice as it relates to leadership scholarship.

Conclusion

As Heifetz and Linsky (2002) so eloquently attest, "the sources of meaning most essential in the human experience draw from our yearning for connection with other people" (p. 209). This is at the heart of leadership development focused on social and political change. Yet, despite this "yearning for connection," the gravity of Western social systems has a tendency to pull us instead toward hyperindividualism—an approach that effectively disrupts opportunities for collective leadership and the pursuit of social justice. An overemphasis on leader development risks exacerbating this. This chapter provides a framework to support educators in advancing the goals of critical and collective leadership development.

References

Boggs, G. L., & Kurashige, S. (2012). *The next American revolution: Sustainable activism for the twenty-first century* (2nd ed.). Berkeley, CA: University of California.

Day, D. V., & Drath, W. (2012). Dialogue: A dialogue on theorizing relational leadership. In M. Uhl-Bien & S. M. Ospina (Eds.), *Advancing relational leadership research: A dialogue among perspectives* (pp. 227–251). Charlotte, NC: Information Age Publishing.

Day, D. V., Harrison, M. M., & Halpin, S. M. (2009). *An integrative approach to leader development: Connecting adult development, identity, and expertise.* New York, NY: Routledge.

Dugan, J. P., & Velázquez, D. (2015). Teaching contemporary leadership: Advancing students' capacities to engage with difference. In S. Watt (Ed.), *Designing transformative multicultural initiatives: Theoretical foundations, practical applications, and facilitator considerations* (pp. 105–118). Sterling, VA: Stylus.

Freire, P. (2000). *Pedagogy of the oppressed.* New York, NY: Bloomsbury Academic.

Gross, J. P. K. (2011). Education and hegemony: The influence of Antonio Gramsci. In B. A. U. Levinson (Ed.), *Beyond critique: Exploring critical social theories and education* (pp. 51–79). Boulder, CO: Paradigm.

Heifetz, R. A., & Linsky, M. (2002). *Leadership on the line: Staying alive through the dangers of leading.* Boston, MA: Harvard Business School Press.

Higher Education Research Institute [HERI]. (1996). *A social change model of leadership development: Guidebook version III.* College Park, MD: National Clearinghouse for Leadership Programs.

Hochschild, J. L. (1995). *Facing up to the American dream: Race, class, and the soul of the nation.* Princeton, NJ: Princeton University Press.

Kezar, A. J., Carducci, R., & Contreras-McGavin, M. (2006). Rethinking the "L" word in higher education: The revolution in research on leadership. *ASHE Higher Education Report, 31*(6). San Francisco, CA: Jossey-Bass.

Komives, S. R., Wagner, W., & Associates. (2009). *Leadership for a better world: Understanding the social change model of leadership development.* San Francisco, CA: Jossey-Bass.

Kumashiro, K. K. (2002). *Troubling education: "Queer" activism and anti-oppressive pedagogy.* New York, NY: Routledge.

Liu, E. (2013). Why ordinary people need to understand power [Video file]. Retrieved from https://www.ted.com/talks/eric_liu_why_ordinary_people_need_to_understand_power?

Noujaim, J. (Director). (2013). *The square* [Motion picture]. United States: Participant Media.

Owen, J. E. (2012). *Findings from the Multi-Institutional Study of Leadership Institutional Survey*. College Park, MD: National Clearinghouse for Leadership Programs.

Preskill, S., & Brookfield, S. D. (2009). *Learning as a way of leading: Lessons from the struggle for social justice*. San Francisco, CA: Jossey-Bass.

Truslow Adams, J. (1931). *The epic of America*. Boston, MA: Little, Brown & Company.

Uhl-Bien, M., & Ospina, S. M. (Eds.). (2012). *Advancing relational leadership research: A dialogue among perspectives*. Charlotte, NC: Information Age Publishing.

Yosso, T. J. (2005). Whose culture has capital? A critical race theory discussion of community cultural wealth. *Race, Ethnicity, and Education, 8*(1), 61–91.

JOHN P. DUGAN is associate professor of higher education at Loyola University Chicago and is principal investigator of the Multi-Institutional Study of Leadership.

NATASHA T. TURMAN and MARK A. TORREZ are doctoral students in higher education at Loyola University Chicago.

2

This chapter describes one university's effort to integrate civic engagement programs and leadership education curriculum, informed by empowerment theory, servant leadership, and community organizing methodologies.

Beyond Service: Equipping Change Agents Through Community Leadership Education

Laurie Marks

Leadership education and community engagement play an important role in how colleges and universities fulfill their civic mission. In the past 20 years there has been a rebirth of both of these enterprises on college campuses (Ehrlich, 2000; Longo & Gibson, 2011). Despite obvious connections between leadership and community engagement, there are few examples in higher education of community leadership education programs that focus on preparing students to facilitate community change. The independent growth of leadership education apart from community-based learning programs leads one to ask, "leadership development for what?" And it has led civic engagement efforts down a path where campuses and students subscribe to a notion of service that is often without reciprocity, lacks a vision of community partners as coeducators, and does little to ensure graduates who are equipped to make systemic change in their communities.

This chapter tells the story of University of Wisconsin–Milwaukee (UWM), an urban institution that changed how community leadership education and civic engagement programs are designed and delivered to the campus and in the community. Structural and philosophical changes were implemented that were informed by empowerment theory, servant leadership, and community organizing methodologies with the end goal of graduating students with strong civic identities oriented toward community action, prepared with collective capacities so essential to leadership for social change. The process will be outlined, and based on the change experience, recommendations are offered.

NEW DIRECTIONS FOR STUDENT LEADERSHIP, no. 148, Winter 2015 © 2015 Wiley Periodicals, Inc., A Wiley Company
Published online in Wiley Online Library (wileyonlinelibrary.com) • DOI: 10.1002/yd.20150

Introduction

After a decade of working in the field of civic engagement and leadership ed-ucation at the University of Wisconsin–Milwaukee (UWM), I began to ask myself some questions about the skill sets and types of leadership identity we were passing along to our students, and how those led to community change. I wondered. Would a student who had spent hundreds of hours tutoring kids at a local public school during his college career know how, later in his life as a parent, to oppose a move to increase class sizes at their own child's school? Would their college experience as a tutor help them to recognize attacks on public education and their ability to ensure positive outcomes for their children and the community? Would they have agency and know how to engage in leadership activities with other parents to fight for funding, and would they know how to examine issues of power in ways that could impact such decisions? Education is just one example; similar questions could be posed around a variety of issues citizens face in their communities related to crime, the environment, public health, and com-munity development.

I wondered. In what ways had we developed empowered citizens through our civic engagement and leadership programs? Were we gradu-ating future community leaders ready to address the challenges faced by our city and its neighborhoods? What parts of the college experience would be called upon to inform how to take community action after they left the institution? Ultimately, I feared they would not take action beyond volun-teerism because we had trained them in a civic identity grounded in direct service without an aim toward deeper change. Over the years I watched as campus programs and seminars focused on specific leadership frameworks (e.g., the social change model or transformational leadership) or specific leadership skills (e.g., time management, public speaking), with little or no connection back to citizen empowerment or community action. Sim-ilarly, community-based learning has largely taken steps toward a service versus action orientation, leaving students disempowered because commu-nity service is presented as the process of filling gaps within agencies by supplementing the work of the nonprofit staff.

In 2011, the UWM campus was at a crossroads, and educators recog-nized an opportunity to provide a more holistic approach to community engagement and community leadership education. This chapter describes how the campus reinvented the way civic engagement and community leadership education is delivered. In this alternative model, community leadership education is delivered in a way that breaks down the barriers between academic and student affairs and takes the elusive concept of empowerment and makes it a concrete developmental process students progress through by way of skill building, reflection, collaboration, critical thinking, power analysis, and an examination of their own civic leadership identity.

New Directions for Student Leadership • DOI: 10.1002/yd

A Void in Community Leadership

The City of Milwaukee suffers from a leadership void, outlined in 2012 by Kurt Chandler in a *Milwaukee Magazine* article, "The Hot Seat." Chandler (2012) asked, "Has civic leadership become too risky? Across the community, observers decry the lack of visionaries willing to lead Milwaukee into the future. Who will take up the challenge?" (p. 35). As Milwaukee and the surrounding region work to combat the negative effects of poverty, racially segregated neighborhoods, high infant mortality, high unemployment rates, educational disparities, and other issues, the void in leadership is palpable. Observers note that few people stand out as change agents; rather, there are overwhelming political divides and many young talented people are choosing to move elsewhere. In that climate, there was an opportunity for UWM to be a place where students could learn a community leadership orientation so that they could be future change agents addressing neighborhood, regional, and statewide issues. UWM is uniquely positioned to have impact in this arena. First, although there are a number of institutions of higher education in the Milwaukee area, 90% of UWM students are Wisconsin residents, and of the 160,000 living alumni, 74% continue to reside in the state. Further, UWM serves a diverse population of students, with the entering freshman class in the fall of 2014 composed of 33% students of color.

To begin the transformation process, the campus administration and governance bodies settled on a series of both structural and philosophical changes to align our program delivery with intended outcomes, campuswide learning goals, and a community-action orientation. The new structure and philosophy are informed by empowerment theory as a developmental pathway, servant leadership as a philosophy, and opportunities for training and reflection on community change and organizing. Further, the campus has embraced a set of shared learning goals based on the American Association of Colleges and Universities (AAC&U) LEAP Initiative, which are congruent with the goals often associated with community leadership and engagement.

Taking Community Engagement to the Next Level: Proposing Radical Structural Changes

The seeds were planted that led to the creation of the Center for Community-Based Learning, Leadership, and Research (CCBLLR) two decades ago. The UWM campus had grown its community engagement profile beginning in the late 1990s, when former Chancellor Nancy Zimpher made financial and institutional commitments to a series of community-based initiatives aimed at the public good, known broadly as the Milwaukee Idea (Zimpher, Percy, & Burkhardt, 2002). The Milwaukee Idea programs became part of the campus identity largely because student, community, and faculty voice were engaged in the building process. This change in campus identity was so deeply rooted that it still is part of the institutional fabric today. The Milwaukee Idea led to specific initiatives, including the establishment of the Institute for Service-Learning, the Center for Volunteerism & Student Leadership, and the Cultures & Communities Certificate Program. This certificate program is a set of courses that allow students to fulfill their general education requirements with a focus on community, civic engagement, multicultural competencies and perspectives, and social action.

For 10 years these three programs grew independently, until 2011, when the fact that they were regularly bumping into one another in the Milwaukee community could no longer be avoided. For example, the university's need for more service-learning placements increased, as did the need for co-curricular volunteer sites. This resulted in different offices within UWM reaching out to the same community partners without the other department's knowledge. Further, the student experience was disjointed, and there was no scaffolding to the community learning journey. Although there were many options to do service in the community and engage in community leadership education, the offerings were not coordinated in terms of scheduling, learning goals, or a centralized physical location on campus to explore the options. Those most closely connected to the civic engagement efforts of the institution acknowledged that there had to be a more holistic approach for students and community partners.

In order to employ a more holistic and developmental approach, the Director of the Center for Volunteerism and Student Leadership, the Director of the Cultures and Communities Program (which oversaw the Institute for Service Learning), and the Chair of the Educational Policy and Community Studies Department brainstormed what a new campus center would offer, and what it would mean to bring particular campus programs together, either administratively or collaboratively. A proposal was written to establish the Center for Community-Based Learning, Leadership, and Research (CCBLLR), whose aim would be to help propel the campus toward four goals. The first was to establish holistic community-based learning and community leadership education programs that met the campus-wide shared learning goals. These included intercultural knowledge and competence, individual, social, and environmental responsibility, and civic knowledge and engagement. The second goal was to strengthen the campus' application for the 2015 Carnegie Classification for Community Engagement. Third, the Center would provide targeted support for UWM faculty and students in community-based research. Finally, the new Center would help UWM graduate more students ready to be active citizens and change agents in neighborhoods across the city and state.

The proposal centered on these goals, and how the impact and experience for the end users (faculty, students, and community partners) would be different under the new centralized model. The proposal suggested a merger of academic and student affairs efforts aimed at community engagement and community leadership education into the new Center for

Community-Based Learning, Leadership, and Research. Broadly, the authors wanted students and community partners to see such programs as multiyear journeys versus a series of disconnected, semester-based opportunities. The campus hoped that by centralizing operations structurally, we could improve the campus profile, increase its impact, and build an interdisciplinary network around community-based initiatives. This is key. UWM was already an engaged campus; however, most community relationships were isolated within departments or dependent on the continued work of particular faculty members. The advent of the new Center brought with it a collaborative energy both on campus and within the city's nonprofit community, thus situating it for the development of collective strategies across sectors in the city and around the campus.

Faculty and administrators involved with civic engagement knew intuitively that consolidating the Center for Volunteerism & Student Leadership with the Institute for Service Learning was an appropriate move, despite the challenge of the common divisional divides found on many campuses between student affairs and academic affairs. The rationale behind the consolidation was sound, because of the nearly 2,000 student placements throughout the city that each office developed independent of the other, but often at the same agencies. Furthermore, there were few service-learning courses offered outside of the College of Letters & Sciences, where the Institute for Service Learning was housed prior to the merger. As a result, there was untapped potential to engage faculty in other colleges interested in exploring service learning as a growing, high-impact, pedagogical practice. Finally, there was not a university-wide sense of what learning outcomes were expected of cocurricular or curricular community leadership education programs, but rather, just a general sense that the campus was deploying a lot of students to do service throughout the city.

Additional Programming to Deepen Student and Faculty Engagement for the Public Good

Once the merger occurred, the new Center for Community-Based Learning, Leadership, and Research developed an extensive menu of community-based initiatives that tracks over 55,000 hours of student community engagement annually. These programs include service-learning support for 90 class sections that enroll over 3,000 students, volunteer programs for hundreds of students serving in the community, a service and leadership scholarship program, leadership development programs, an alternative spring break service trip, and 75 community-based work–study jobs with placements at public schools and local nonprofits. Additionally, there were two initiatives added beyond what the merger of the offices brought to the table, and both proved to play a key role in reaching the campus goals.

First, a Community Engaged Scholars Network (CESN) was established for faculty and researchers, which quickly grew to nearly 200 members. The CESN holds well-attended events a few times each semester where members discuss interdisciplinary community research projects, best practices in service learning, funding opportunities, and community needs they become aware of in their work but are outside of their particular expertise. This network provides faculty with a peer group of other engaged scholars, a context for the larger campus commitment to community work being done, and serves as a symbol to community leaders and campus administrators that the civic mission of the campus is important to the faculty.

A second initiative was to connect a series of both curricular and cocurricular leadership programs to the new Center. One, for example, was an 18-credit community leadership certificate program offered through the School of Education with specific coursework in leadership theory and community organizing, and a practicum in the community. This certificate program provides students who are energized by a volunteer or service-learning experience with a next step through a university-guided program with a focus on community leadership. Similarly, an alternative path is a cocurricular option called the Emerging Leaders Program. In this program students take only one credit-bearing leadership course, with remaining requirements fulfilled by cocurricular work including an internship, a community mentor relationship, an overnight retreat, and a series of other community experiences designed by the student based on their interest. The new Center serves as a hub for engagement and community leadership education by erasing the structural lines that campuses routinely draw between departments and administrative divisions—lines that have very little meaning to students and community partners. Eliminating these lines provides the opportunity to scaffold experiences with deeper reach and a more holistic approach to community leadership development.

Student Civic Identity Development Informed by Empowerment Theory and Servant Leadership Philosophy

Although the structural changes were informed by the logistical needs of students, faculty, and community partners, program goals and content were driven by leadership and engagement philosophies associated with community action, including empowerment theory. Empowerment theory focuses on individual and organizational strengths versus weaknesses, and allows communities to improve the overall well-being of their environment through democratic participation in social and political change efforts (Rappaport, 1984). Although an often misunderstood concept, empowerment can include components such as self-definition, an understanding of one's personal connection to sociopolitical issues, and a group's ability to organize around common community goals (Sadan, 2004). From a developmental perspective, empowerment theory can provide an outline of how students may grow in their beliefs and skills related to community action, bridging the gap between being of service and an agent for change. For many new college students, this is a difficult leap because it requires an un-learning of what community engagement means. As more K–12 programs and religious organizations encourage or require service, students arrive as freshman with an expectation that they will do service; however, it is from a volunteer perspective. This disassociates the student from the issues around them, creates a counterproductive power dynamic between them and those they interact with at service-learning sites, and does little to train them to make systemic change.

Often community engagement and community leadership programs focus solely on critical thinking and reflection, or on specific leadership skills, but rarely on both, and even more rarely are the two explicitly connected in a community context for students. The skills gained when community engagement occurs alongside coursework should prepare students to examine issues of power, community impact, and leadership identities. However, the experiences have to be coupled with not only critical thinking exercises and reflection, but also with opportunities for active listening, relationship building, mentorship, public speaking, power analysis, and coalition building. Because this list of skills and experiences is too complex to learn in a semester or single experience, leadership development must provide progressively more in-depth and complex opportunities and experiences that allow students to engage regularly in the community during one's college career. This ongoing engagement is more likely to lead to community action, issue organizing, or other practices that focus on systemic impact.

Ideally, graduates should practice integrated learning or be able to call up the experiences from their college career that inform community action. For example, consider the profile described at the start of this chapter of the student who spent hundreds of hours tutoring kids at a local school, only to be paralyzed by inaction when after graduating, funding for his own child's school was cut. A component of their civic engagement should include an examination of issues around school funding, as well as community organizing tactics and methods. If we provided this additional component to the community engagement experience, then that student might also have learned how to negotiate with people of differing points of view, and how to build a coalition of concerned parents and citizens.

Kieffer (1984) offers an empowerment developmental model that can be applied to student civic identity development. The model suggests that individuals go through four eras, including the era of entry, the era of advancement, the era of incorporation, and the era of commitment (Kieffer, 1984). Initially one begins with few competencies and little confidence that they can create change, and moves toward an understanding of one's own skills and the collective power of a community (Kieffer, 1984). Because this process could not happen in a semester, campuses have to be intentional about providing opportunities to experience some of the key components in each of the eras to students over the course of a few years.

In the era of entry, one becomes aware of an issue or event that violates their rights or sense of control over their environment, which then necessitates the need for a community organizing skill set. One of the aims of service learning in university settings is to help students integrate into the geographic community in which the campus exists. In this phase students need to feel a personal connection and stake in community issues, and the work they are doing at service-learning sites provides this opportunity. Students who engage in youth development work as tutors or mentors, for example, may not automatically make this connection to themselves or the larger issues; rarely do they ever ask why the schools in Milwaukee need so many tutors in the first place. They are willing to serve, but they are not prompted to ask these critical questions, which leads to the bigger question of how to organize families and communities so that the needs for tutoring and volunteering are diminished.

However, when faculty members have visited service-learning sites, they are quick to observe and problematize such topics, and can bring these discussions back to the classroom. We can challenge students to think about how overcrowded classrooms in public schools in low-income neighborhoods might impact their own urban experience. What if they choose to stay in the city when they graduate? Where will their kids attend school? How does inequity in education negatively impact citizens regionally, including those who move to the suburbs? In the nomenclature of community organizing, students need to recognize their self-interest, versus approaching engagement from a do-good-for-others mindset. Community organizing practice is informed by empowerment theory and can be described as a process whereby people of a particular community work together to make change within the community based on identified self-interest. This is the frame by which community leadership and service learning should begin— that students are part of these communities, and have a self-interest in the issues.

Many service-learning and volunteer program managers describe how transportation is one of the primary barriers for students. Besides the logistics related to utilizing public transportation, there are other challenges, such as the fear students feel about navigating unfamiliar urban neighborhoods. The Center for Community-Based Learning, Leadership, and Research made a conscious choice to tackle this issue head-on. We invested in a van to transport students to particular volunteer and service-learning locations, and instituted a Van Chat program that utilizes the travel time to have peer-led discussions about students' experiences at the site. These conversations are critical; otherwise, students are being chauffeured to sites, without understanding the context in which their service is being done, especially in cocurricular programs where there is not a facilitated discussion in a classroom after the experience. Van Chats pose progressively more complex questions to student riders each week about their own life experiences and what they are learning about the lives of those at the community-based learning sites. Students discuss how they observe issues of race and poverty along the route and at the site, how they see their service as having an impact, and how their service might in fact reinforce existing structures that do not serve community members well. Quick van rides show students just how geographically close poverty is to the campus community, whereas long bus rides that are not actually many miles away, but require transfers and lots of stops, can reinforce a sense of those neighborhoods for students, and will often prevent students from participating altogether.

As students progress through the era of advancement, it is important that campus officials work alongside community partners to ensure that students experience "mentorship and supportive peer relationships within collective organizational structure" (Kieffer, 1984, p. 20). This generally comes from other service learners, clients at sites, staff, or community volunteers engaging in the work. One of the challenges for faculty incorporating service learning into a course is the lack of control of the learning environment and recognizing community partners as coeducators. To alleviate this problem, syllabi and course readings should be shared with community partners, and discussions should occur about how experiences at the service site will enhance learning. These relationships can help foster a critical comprehension of social and political issues associated with the service-learning tasks and projects, and may lead to students staying on at sites beyond their required course hours. Even when community agencies do not engage in community organizing directly, staff often have an understanding for the need for systemic change, and can pass it on to students while they supervise them at placement sites.

At a recent meeting with faculty from three different departments, and a nonprofit leader from an agency that assists children with disabilities, the Executive Director explained that her agency had for 17 years provided services to teach families how to navigate systems that served children. Now, however, they needed to make a shift, and instead teach families how to change systems. Working collectively to alter relations of power is often how citizens experience community leadership, and agencies engaged in such work provide an aspect of leadership education we rarely see in the classroom. Giving students the opportunity to reflect on issues of community control and power will allow them to explore power dichotomies between themselves and the community members at service-learning sites and overall systems within communities. These settings share a characteristic in that they have "… structures, norms, and practices, providing opportunity for and contribute to member development and change" (Maton, 2008, p. 8). The faculty members at this meeting had different levels of understanding and interest in this idea of shift from navigating systems to changing systems. Yet overall, they understood that when service learners from their classes were placed at this site, they would be providing services to families, and observing how the agency was working to change systems.

Next, the era of incorporation is associated with greater self-concept in the larger context of leadership and community skills, and one's ongoing growth related to social and political issues (Kieffer, 1984). Many campuses promote models of community leadership education aimed at transformation: the social change model, transformational leadership, shared leadership, and servant leadership. What we do not always do well is to bridge the two arenas of leadership and civic identity. How do students who have engaged in service learning, and have also learned about the 7 Cs of the social change model of leadership development, for example, learn to integrate the two for tangible community impact? The social change model focuses on collaboration among stakeholders, citizenship, consciousness of self, congruence in one's actions, a common purpose, commitment to issues, and controversy with civility (Komives, Wagner, & Associates, 2009). However, when we define *collaboration* or *controversy with civility* to students, can they understand the concepts beyond the neat framework presented in a PowerPoint or even when presented in a case study? It is difficult to learn the nuances of stakeholder collaboration until you have engaged in a community meeting where issues have been debated or you have watched organizations with different missions work together on neighborhood programs. The era of incorporation is present when students are actively integrating their skills, interests, and ideas into particular agencies, issues, and neighborhoods from social and political perspectives. This allows students to experience other aspects of development commonly associated with this phase, such as personal conflicts related to the knowledge they develop, their values, and new skills at addressing community issues (Kieffer, 1984).

In the final phase, the era of commitment, individuals continue to wrestle with their own growth, skills, and awareness of political issues, while continuing to integrate their identity into community work (Kieffer, 1984). Utilizing the tenants of servant leadership, for example, can help students to integrate such work into their long-term civic identity. Servant leadership is characterized by ideas such as being of service first; being committed to the growth of others; active listening; working to lift up members of the community who are more vulnerable; and most importantly, working toward personal, organizational, and societal change (Northouse, 2013). Ultimately we want students, regardless of their major or career path, to adopt a leadership identity that incorporates servant leadership into their professional and community lives. When service-learning, university-coordinated volunteer work, or leadership development programs are not tied to a student's field of study, community interests, and future goals, it becomes more challenging for students to see community engagement as part of who they are, because it's an add-on.

At larger universities where there are significant numbers of service learners to be placed, direct service placements that reinforce doing for others versus creating change are unavoidable. Often the identified community need that agencies present to those that build campus/community partnerships is direct service. This dynamic presents a challenge to our goals to teach students community leadership skills from a change perspective versus a service-to-others perspective. Further, students are usually not ready to be change agents, as many of them bring their high school definition and understanding of service with them; a certain number of hours aimed at doing something for, versus with, members of the community. To overcome this challenge, the Center for Community-Based Learning, Leadership, and Research actively discusses these goals with organizations that may deliver direct service, but have a community-change orientation. These settings share a characteristic in that they have "... structures, norms and practices, providing opportunity for and contribute to member development and change" (Maton, 2008, p. 8).

For example, UWM's School of Architecture and Urban Planning offers a service-learning course called Architecture 350: Greening Milwaukee. Last year students from this course worked alongside middle and high school students from Escuela Verde, a local nontraditional school that utilizes a project-based curriculum. Together, grounded in the idea that the kids at the school knew best what their optimal learning environment would be, UWM architecture students helped them design a new learning space. Escuela Verde's mission reflects the belief that youth who will be in the space should be a part of the design process; educators wanted their students to feel empowered as their school moved to a new location. This is one example in which UWM students work with, not for, and learned from those at a community partner site.

How community-based learning assignments are structured to explore these issues is critical, and needs to be coordinated on the faculty end as well as with the community organization. As a university we explore how we can share this vision of educating students to be future change agents with our partners and their clients. We ask them how they see themselves as coeducators, sharing their knowledge and experience working directly in the community, and offer insight that those on campus may not have related to community impact and issue organizing.

Recommendations to Move Beyond Service

Creating a deliberate developmental path for students to become change agents is critical to successful community leadership education. At UWM there were a series of moves required to ensure this shift. First, we subscribe to community *action* versus community *service* as a community leadership philosophy. In order to do this, we need to address community needs while building strategic partnerships between the university and nonprofit agencies where staff have a social change orientation. Through this orientation we can shine light on issues of power in relationships as a recognized aspect of leadership and community engagement. This may occur in the classroom for service learners, or while student volunteers talk during peer-led Van

Chats. As a campus we can role model shared power, shared decisions, and how the community is embraced as a coeducator.

In the field of campus/community partnership, the concept of equitable relationships is often identified as a goal. Many partner institutions have varying resources in terms of technology, people, and money, and so an acknowledgment of this is a way to demonstrate power differentials as a part of student learning. This is a departure of the language we currently use, suggesting that we can create equal partnerships between admittedly unequal entities. Teaching students about power structures in community-based learning settings, and how they influence services, community member identities, missions, and staff at agencies is important.

Second, we can expose students to the larger public policy issues that bring them to the community partner sites, and embrace the controversy that often comes with these issues as opportunities for student learning. Recently I attended an orientation for a group of 35 UWM students who were about to begin tutoring children at a public school in one of the most economically disadvantaged neighborhoods in Wisconsin. In the middle of the orientation, a short debate broke out among the trainers. The community volunteer that led the training made a case against standardized testing and No Child Left Behind mandates. A teacher who was also there provided an alternative view, explaining why she supported the law. That 7 minutes may have been as informative to our students as the following months of tutoring; students heard about some of the larger policy issues facing educators and children, they witnessed two people with differing opinions engage in debate around a shared purpose, and they saw firsthand some of the expertise held by the community.

Third, we can create methods for explaining community context and history to students who are regularly engaged at local nonprofit agencies. The history and context allow students to see neighborhoods from an asset versus deficit perspective, meaning they see the value that exists in a community instead of only its shortcomings; this can provide students with a deeper understanding of community members, who have simply had different life experiences. Most important, it can demonstrate to students their stake in the success of the larger community versus just the one organization or issue with which they identify. The best way to provide community context for students is to recognize community members as coeducators. To model how educators at the university see the importance of empowerment, we must be willing to trust that community partners will wrestle with and find ways to provide meaningful educational experiences during critical episodes that occur at service-learning sites. One of the ways that some UWM courses have done this successfully is by having students who are engaged in project-based service-learning work attend resident/neighbor meetings or work alongside staff outside of the particular project they are working on so that they experience the culture of the agency, gain a sense of the neighborhood, and develop relationships with group leaders.

Fourth, it is important to engage students in formative reflection instead of relying solely upon summative reflection as they progress along the developmental path in particular service-learning courses, and during their college career. This means regularly checking in with students through writing assignments or small group discussion instead of only requiring final project at a semester's end. Students must be asked throughout the experience to articulate their own community leadership identity and philosophy, explore and articulate how they are a part of communities they do service in, what areas ignite them in terms of personal interest, and what skills they have or need that contribute to leading change. This is only done by marrying civic engagement and community leadership education programs from a structural and philosophical perspective, one that provides a holistic approach resulting in skilled community change agents. As we redesigned and restructured our programs, we kept asking ourselves, "what does the experience look like from a student and community partner perspective?" For example, when a student takes a service-learning course, and then the next year volunteers at a university-sponsored youth mentoring program, and in all four years of college participates in an alternative spring break program, are they directed and engaged in four different departments with four different ideas about community leadership? Often this difficult task of scaffolding experiences and synthesizing how it all might impact one's identity is left to students without much coordinated guidance across different program areas.

Finally, consider the reach, length, and depth of community engagement efforts beyond simply the number of students involved. While some campuses move toward a community service requirement, I would challenge administrators to consider the impact of such short-term requirements on students and the community. Rather, if our campus can teach many students, but not all, the value of sustained relationships with communities beyond one semester, it is more likely that we will have nurtured future leaders prepared to face complex issues. Creating a culture of sustained relationships between particular students, neighborhoods, faculty, and the nonprofit agencies deepens student learning, can lead to faculty research projects, and has greater impact in the community.

Rather than making a university-wide student requirement for civic engagement, campuses should focus resources on expanding service learning to unlikely departments on campus, especially those in the professional schools. Most campuses have specific departments that are more inclined to engage in service learning as a pedagogical practice. As public and private institutions of higher education seek to show their relevance to citizens and politicians, community engagement and community leadership education are an avenue that resonates with the general public. Within campus departments there are faculty experts who can build relationships with community partners around project-based service-learning work that will provide community partners with tangible tools that may increase the groups capacity. Campuses should seize this moment to build new and innovative relationships with colleagues and new community partners to collaborate on projects aimed at the public good.

Conclusion

It can be difficult to ensure students have an opportunity to explore the assets they bring to service sites, which at first glance may seem minimal. Often students will eagerly sign up to work with low-income families for example, only to be hit early on with the reality that they do not have the skills needed to work across race, class, and culture, which can be unsettling and makes them feel out of place. It is these crossroads where students learn how pervasive issues related to poverty can be, and they begin to think about how their field of study might tackle them, and what tangential skills they do possess that might impact communities. Often agency staff look to young people to mentor near-age clients, promote the agency name through social media, create digital stories through YouTube videos, or bring other skills to the table. Students need space to build relationships and then reflect on what skills they have, what skills they will develop, and which they will need to in order to make change.

Each day I am amazed by students and faculty doing community work at my institution because in many ways this work is harder and more time consuming than traditional classroom-based education. Community-minded scholars face a tough challenge, as the culture of higher education is still somewhat inwardly focused, often bureaucratic in nature, and does not adequately value or reward community-engaged scholarship. These aspects of our professional culture push against community-based learning and community leadership education. Further, we exist in an environment with experts in many fields, and we ask them to turn over some control of the student learning experience to the community partners in erratic and uncontrolled environments such as crowded public schools, busy nonprofits, and neighborhoods with economic challenges. But this is often the most valuable and real-world learning environment we can provide for students.

Recently, a woman from a nonprofit organization approached me while she was on our campus for an event called Communities in the Round, where she was doing an on-campus orientation with a group of service-learning students enrolled in a Conservation and Environmental Science class. She explained that while in college at UWM 6 years earlier she struggled academically, was unsure of what to do, and had little focus. It was the same class and event 6 years earlier that was a game-changer for her, and she then knew she wanted to be a leader in the nonprofit environmental community. As a result, she was able to focus her academic work, graduate, and have a fulfilling career. Those working in this field hear this regularly while out on site visits, and it is easy to feel good about it, and mentally pat ourselves on the back. But what I really wanted to ask her was if we had given her the tools to make systemic change, and if her experience as a service learner exposed her at all to the public policy issues related to the environment. My sense is that this is the next step in evolution of civic engagement and community leadership education.

References

Chandler, K. (2012). The hot seat. *Milwaukee Magazine, 37*, 34–42.

Ehrlich, T. (Ed.). (2000). *Civic responsibility in higher education.* Phoenix, AZ: Oryx Press.

Kieffer, C. (1984). Citizen empowerment: A developmental perspective. *Prevention in Human Services, 3*(2), 9–36.

Komives, S. R., Wagner, W., & Associates. (2009). *Leadership for a better world: Understanding the social change model of leadership development.* San Francisco, CA: Jossey Bass.

Longo, N. V., & Gibson, C. M. (Eds.). (2011). *From command to community: A new approach to leadership education in colleges and universities.* Medford, MA: Tufts University Press.

Maton, K. I. (2008). Empowering community settings: Agents of individual development, community betterment, and positive social change. *American Journal of Community Psychology, 41*, 4–21.

Northouse, P. G. (2013). *Leadership: Theory and practice.* Thousand Oaks, CA: Sage.

Rappaport, J. (1984). Studies in empowerment: Introduction to the issue. In J. Rappaport, C. Swift, & R. Hess (Eds.), *Studies in empowerment: Steps toward understanding and action* (pp. 1–8). New York, NY: Haworth Press.

Sadan, E. (2004). *Empowerment and community planning* (R. Flantz, Trans.). Tel Aviv, Israel: Hakibbutz Hameuchad.

Zimpher, N., Percy, S. L., & Burkhardt, M. J. (2002). *A time for boldness: A story of institutional change.* Bolton, MA: Anker.

LAURIE MARKS is the executive director of the UW-Milwaukee University Center for Community-Based Learning, Leadership and Research.

3

This chapter describes how present conditions in Black communities have fostered the development of new modes of youth leadership that focus on hope, love, and joy, and are ultimately restorative and redemptive.

Radically Healing Black Lives: A Love Note to Justice

Shawn A. Ginwright

The air in Tanisha's apartment was thick and humid, like the air outside. The small fan in her bedroom did little to cool the mammoth heat that had covered Jennings, Missouri. She was running late for work this morning. In fact, she had to force herself out of bed, and felt guilty about not wanting to explain to her classroom of eighth graders at Gateway Middle School why the world had descended on their neighborhood with bright lights, news cameras, and trucks with big satellite dishes pointing up to the sky. Despite the fact that she was tired from the march and late-night community meeting about the events in nearby Ferguson, she washed her face, slid on her jeans, and buttoned up her yellow short sleeve blouse. She headed to school to teach her 30 eager eighth grade students the most important lesson they would ever learn in school: why their lives really mattered.

Tanisha, along with thousands of other citizens, joined the protests in Ferguson, MO, to help bring worldwide attention to the police shooting of unarmed Michael Brown. She had grown frustrated by the ways in which the news had portrayed the protestors, and admittedly she was somewhat naïve about how the police treated Black citizens in the area. She joined her friends and thousands of other protesters expressing their moral outrage about a justice system that sanctioned the murder of an unarmed citizen. She expected a peaceful protest, but just after 9:15 p.m., her group was ordered by police to disperse. Without notice the police, decked out in their military regalia, unleashed tear gas, flash grenades, and dogs on her group of friends. She was terrified, and at that moment she knew that her life would never be the same. Instantly, her fear had transformed itself into righteous indignation, and blossomed in her an uncompromised love for

NEW DIRECTIONS FOR STUDENT LEADERSHIP, no. 148, Winter 2015 © 2015 Wiley Periodicals, Inc., A Wiley Company
Published online in Wiley Online Library (wileyonlinelibrary.com) • DOI: 10.1002/yd.20151

justice. When she arrived at school the next morning, she smiled at her colleagues, waved to parents, and happily greeted each child as if she had never smelled the burning fear of tear gas in her eyes, and nostrils. But when she entered her classroom with her freshly pressed yellow blouse, she explained to her students that America was broken, and together they could fix it.

This chapter is about the convergence of love and justice, and examines how young leaders of color are expanding conventional modes of civic engagement in order to assert human dignity collectively. This chapter illustrates how present conditions in Black communities have fostered new modes of leadership that focus on hope, love, and joy and are ultimately restorative and redemptive. With the use of the radical healing framework, this chapter explores how the campaign #Blacklivesmatter represents a growing movement for healing justice in Black life.

Why Black Lives Matter

In the months after an officer shot and killed unarmed Michael Brown, there were numerous other cases of unarmed Black men, boys, and women killed by White police officers across the country, including Ezell Ford in California; John Crawford, Tamir Rice, and Tanisha Anderson in Ohio; and Eric Garner and Akai Gurley in New York. Over the past 2 years, the country has been riveted to social media, radio, and television to learn about accounts of police shootings of unarmed citizens. On July 13, 2013, a jury found George Zimmerman not guilty of homicide for shooting the unarmed teen Trayvon Martin. Ironically, on July 12, a day before the Zimmerman verdict, the film *Fruitvale Station* (Coogler, 2013) was released, depicting the life and humanity of Oscar Grant, a young man fatally shot by police officers after stepping off a Bay Area Rapid Transit train in Oakland. A little over a year later, on July 17, 2014, Eric Garner was choked to death in broad daylight by a New York City police officer. Again the officer was not indicted. Almost a month later on August 9, 2014, Michael Brown, an unarmed African American teen, was shot and killed by a police officer. A grand jury was not convinced that there was sufficient evidence to indict the officer. Thousands of people—a multiracial coalition of gay, straight, poor, and wealthy—were outraged, not so much about the specifics involved in each of these cases, but about who we have become as a society. Thousands of people asked questions about America's moral compass in regards to the lives of African American young men and women.

Unlike other forms of collective action in the past (e.g., the Occupy protests of 2011–2012) that begin with the general public's moral outrage, compel thousands to take to the streets, and spark disruption in the calm daily lives of citizens, these recent protests are different. These mass mobilizations, consisting of thousands of young people from around the world, seem to be pushed by moral outrage and pulled by a love ethic. A love ethic is an unconditional desire for human dignity, meaningful existence, and hope. #Blacklivesmatter is a movement of dignity, meaning, and hope in a critical moment when race in general, and Blackness in particular, has become a third rail, and avoided in policy debates. The statement "Black lives matter" also gives others permission to practice courageous love and to celebrate and protect the dignity and humanity of all people. The #Blacklivesmatter campaign is rooted in an understanding that in order for everyone to enjoy the fruits of civic engagement, the dignity and humane treatment of Black young men, women, families, and communities must be central to our political analysis, organizing strategies, and policy solutions.

Unlike the mass Civil Rights Movements of the 20th century that ushered in groundbreaking legislation, today's events require new modes of organizing that are both inwardly focused on meaning making and healing from the wounds inflicted from structural oppression, as well as outwardly focused on social change (Ginwright, 2010). This dual focus represents a new way of movement building by engaging a collective conversation about the power of hope and the meaning it holds for each of us. Young community leaders increasingly acknowledge that both organizing and healing together are required for lasting community change. Both strategies, braided together, make a more complete and durable fabric in our efforts to transform oppression, and hold the power to restore a more humane, and redemptive process toward community change.

Challenges to Black Organizing and Youth Leadership

African American communities in the post–civil-rights era have dramatically changed. Crack cocaine, caste-like poverty, the diminishment of living-wage jobs, and the lack of state intervention have eroded an important political and activist infrastructure in Black communities. The dramatic changes in Black political and civic life have perhaps had the greatest impact on Black youth. Where once there was a vibrant civic and political life among Black youth in the Civil Rights and Black Power movements through organizations like SNCC, Black Panther Party, and CORE, today civic life and political engagement for Black youth is threatened by the inability of organizations to confront some of the most pressing issues facing Black youth. Organizations like the NAACP, National Urban League, Links, and other organizations that traditionally played a significant role in the development of political leadership have been unable to grapple with the issues facing African American communities. These changes in Black community life have created three barriers to Black activism and leadership in the post–civil-rights era. Together these barriers continue to threaten the capacity of effective organizing in Black communities.

Lack of a Black Organizing Infrastructure. Since the 1970s community organizations dedicated to activism have experienced a steady decline (Jenkins, 1995; McAdam, 1982; Piven & Cloward, 1979). This decline can largely be attributed to (a) the growth and expansion of government and nonprofit social support services in African American communities, (b) the stigma of activism and organizing following the attacks on organizing by COINTELPRO and other assaults on Black activism, and (c) lack of resources for building the capacity for Black organizing. Together these factors have marginalized organizing as a meaningful and effective tool for community change (Churchill & Vander Wall, 2002).

For example, in late 1990s, communities throughout the country saw a dramatic expansion for strategies that included youth organizing. The Ford Foundation's leadership expanded the terrain for numerous other foundations to follow suit and support youth organizing. Although Black organizing occupied only a fraction of the philanthropic resources, there were key efforts that contributed to a burgeoning Black organizing infrastructure consisting of key organizations, annual training and convenings, and opportunities to share best practices among youth organizers. This period of philanthropic attention, however, was short lived. I recall the comments of one program officer at the Ford Foundation, who stated in a meeting, "the revolution will not be funded." She was correct, and as a result very little philanthropic attention has been focused on organizing since the early 2000s. The lack of investment in organizing has limited the available pathways for new Black activists to enter organizing work, and the places where African American activists convene, share lessons, and learn about organizing efforts.

Fragmentation and Isolation. There are a number of tensions that complicate organizing in African American communities. First are the growing class tensions between educated professional and working poor communities. These tensions, while rarely discussed publicly, have fostered different and sometime conflicting views on how to address pressing issues. Although some view community organizing and building power among constituents as an important strategy to change unjust policies, others focus almost entirely on political power and voting as the secret sauce to social change. Although it is true that this is false separation, these issues have made it difficult to close ranks and coalesce around a common agenda.

The significance of #Blacklivesmatter in some ways bridges this gap because, rather than only focusing on a specific policy, like stop and frisk, it calls for an overarching appeal to basic human dignity. Although the movement has been criticized for its lack of strategy to achieve policy goals regarding policing practices, it provides meaning and the framing necessary for collective action. #Blacklivesmatter allows us to interpret and assign specific meaning to injustice and collectively act to bring about desired social change. Snow and Benford (2000) have labeled the process of interpreting and assigning meaning to social issues as collective action framing. Collective action frames allow individuals to simplify and interpret the complex social world in ways that are meaningful, and functions to organize belief systems that encourage collective action (Benford & Snow,

2000; Goffman, 1974). Building from Goffman (1974), Benford and Snow (2000) argued that frames "are action-oriented sets of beliefs and meanings that inspire and legitimate" social movement activities (p. 614). Snow and Benford (1988) later argued that successful mobilization is contingent upon "its ability to affect both consensus and action mobilization" (p. 199), which can be achieved through specific framing processes.

Lack of Meaning and Hope. Growing challenges in Black communities such as violence, substance abuse, joblessness, and lack of trust have become increasingly toxic to vibrant community life. Leaders of color have expressed that one of the greatest challenges facing social justice work is the growing sense of spiritual emptiness and burnout. These issues, as earlier discussed in Chapter 1, "Beyond individual leader development: Cultivating collective capacities," can result in activists who leave social justice work altogether, or who simply lose faith in organizing as a tool for social change. Creating and sustaining social justice movements require intense dedication and commitment that often breed burnout, which in turn fosters loss of purpose. Activist Yashna Maya Padamsee (2011) observes:

> We put our bodies on the line everyday—because we care so deeply about our work—hunger strikes, long marches, long days at the computer, or long days organizing on a street corner, or a public bus, or a congregation. Skip a meal, keep working. Don't sleep, keep working. Our communities are still suffering, so I must keep going. (para. 10)

These challenges to African American youth leadership organizing are even more difficult with policies that restrict, control, and contain young people. For example, police departments' stop-and-frisk practices and zero-tolerance policies in schools disproportionately criminalize young men of color for willful defiance and all have negative impact on young people's social emotional health (Center on Juvenile and Criminal Justice, 1999). Young people in urban settings who have fallen prey to these discriminatory practices often have few opportunities to address the psychosocial harm resulting from persistent exposure to an ecosystem of violence. Their experiences are not only traumatizing, but often have a profoundly negative impact on their sense of efficacy and agency.

This means that we have to view structural issues such as poverty, unemployment, underfunded schools, incarceration, lack of access to quality health care, and poor-quality housing as representing a collective experience shared by young people, and their families. These structural issues contribute to socially toxic environments (Garbarino, 1995). Environments where lack of opportunities, blocked access, constrained resources, and unclear pathways to a better life can erode trusting relationships, and severely constrain agency required for collective action (Ginwright, 2010). Paul Farmer (2004) called this structural violence, where structural oppression destroys and harms communities. He accurately highlighted the ways in which racism, homophobia, classism, sexism, and other forms of systemic exclusion are embedded in social institutions and harm communities and groups in our society.

Leadership, Love, and Healing Justice

These barriers require a new strategy to revive the vibrant leadership and organizing potential within Black communities. In Black communities ravaged by violence, crime, and poverty, organizing is often created and sustained by building healing communities where individuals restore a sense of hope, and possibilities for community change. Healing justice is an emerging movement that seeks both (a) collective healing and well-being, and also (b) transforming the institutions and relationships that are causing the harm in the first place (Wallace, 2012). This transformation requires us to address the ways that social institutions and policies harm more than help, while simultaneously building practices in communities that promote well-being. As such, healing justice focuses on both the systemic consequences of oppression on hope and how communities can heal and be restored to vibrant, healthy communities. Healing justice practitioners are acutely aware of the ways in which stress, lack of resources, violence, and prolonged exposure to trauma, all present tremendous challenges in creating community and/or social change. Similar to environmental justice activists, who view policies that harm the earth as political issues, healing justice activists view policies that harm individual and community well-being as political as well. For example, environmental justice activists view policies that promote pollution and fossil fuels as harmful to the earth and our environment. Much of their activism focuses on protecting the environment from harm created by lack of awareness or concern for the natural environment. Similarly, healing justice activists view policies that promote violence, stress, hopelessness in schools and communities, as harmful to our collective well-being, human dignity, and hope. Rather than viewing well-being as an individual act of self-care, healing justice advocates view the practice of healing as political action.

Nicole Lee (2014), Executive Director of Urban Peace Movement in Oakland, CA, commented that we often think of social change occurring from the top down (i.e., government programs), or from the bottom up (i.e., grassroots community organizing). However, the conditions in urban communities of color also require that we address the long-term exposure to social trauma. This means social change from the inside out by working on self-transformation, healing, hopefulness, and fostering a general sense of well-being. By and large, these practices do not exist in urban schools and community organizations, as we now know them. As a result, their absence has been the Achilles heel of modern organizing's effort to engage constituencies in a deeper way. Inside-out social change simply means examining both the root causes of barriers to building effective, healthy, and vibrant communities, and focusing on caring for our collective mental and physical health. Healing justice advocates examine the process that contributes to individual well-being, community health, and broader social justice.

Lee is a long-time community organizer in Oakland. After years of front-line organizing, she recognized that healing from years of exposure to toxic public policy was also key for community change. She commented that sometimes she wondered if the young people of color would be able to absorb the benefits of the policy wins for which they worked. In her poignant paper on healing-centered organizing, she wrote,

> I heard environmental author Paul Hawken use the metaphor of a healthy watershed in a speech about creating sustainable local economies. He said that in a healthy watershed, fertile soil absorbs rain when it falls, and the rain feeds the whole ecosystem. The local environment flourishes as a result. However, environmental degradation has left many places around the world with dry, cracked soil. In these places, the rains seldom come. But, even when they do, the soil is so damaged that it can't absorb the rain. The water runs off elsewhere. Hawken described this as a metaphor to illustrate issues surrounding local economies, but I found it just as helpful when thinking about my work with Oakland's young people. I wondered and worried whether the youth I worked with would be ready to take whatever green jobs we helped create. Did they even know what a "green job" was or why it was important? I came to understand that. .. the policy wins that we seek are the rain, and the youth are the soil. The soil has to be tended to and cared for so that it can absorb the rain. (Lee, 2012, p. 7)

Increasingly, social change youth leaders are focusing on ways for other young people to absorb the rain, or heal so that they enjoy benefits of policy wins. #Blacklivesmatter is one example of healing justice because it highlights three important features of the healing justice framework, which are restoration, resistance, and reclamation.

Restoration.   The first feature, restoration, involves actions and activities that restore collective well-being, meaning, and purpose. Restoration in this sense is a political act because it recognizes the collective nature of well-being, and moves away from individualistic notions of health, and views restoration of community as the result of political power agency, voice, and action.

#Blacklivesmatter activists share a common awareness of restoration as an important political and organizing strategy. For example, after the slogan #Blacklivesmatter spread like wild fire across the media, into political commentary, throughout popular blogs, BLM activists were asked shift the slogan to "Alllivesmatter" to capture the essence of how other groups embraced the term. BLM activists rejected the intentional diminishing of "Black" in the phrase. Their rejection called attention to how other progressive groups viewed the term *Black* as alienating and divisive. The

#Blacklivesmatter movement is unapologetically Black, choosing to embrace the term "Black lives," which restores a healthy, holistic, and purposeful placement of Blackness into meaningful political action and discourse.

Resistance.   The second feature is resistance, which involves disrupting and rejecting hegemonic notions of justice, particularly in regards to race. One example from the #Blacklivesmatter movement occurred in December, 2014. Fourteen #Blacklivesmatter protestors brought the entire Bay Area Rapid Transit system to a halt when they formed a human chain through a BART train and locked themselves to the West Oakland BART platform. Their protest appeared on blog posts and news outlets, and called attention to how the comfort of our routines rarely require us to question issues of justice. The passengers sat for nearly an hour before the trains restarted. These protests among young people are eloquent acts of resistance, and point to the inextricable connection between power and well-being. Well-being is a function of control and power young people have in their schools and communities (Morsillo & Prilleltensky, 2007; Prilleltensky & Prilleltensky, 2006). Resistance among #Blacklivesmatter protestors signals an important source of hope, a necessary ingredient to social change.

Reclamation.   The third feature of radical healing is reclamation, the capacity to reclaim, redefine, and reimagine a possible future. The #Blacklivesmatter movement is more than a hashtag, and is reclaiming Black organizing by departing from conventional tropes of the Civil Rights Movements. In fact, Alicia Garza, one of the initial founders of the movement, commented in a recent speech that #Blacklivesmatter is not the new Civil Rights Movement, but rather a movement of our time, on our terms, for our issues (Stelzer, 2015). We should pay attention to the innovative leadership and innovations in movement building. One only needs to recall the events of the Arab Spring in 2010 that toppled the Egyptian government in part by using social media to communicate and organize thousands of young people. Similarly, #Blacklivesmatter has ruptured the static civil rights modes of protests that focus on mass demonstration, taking dissent to cyberspace. By deploying social media technology like Twitter, Facebook, Tumblr, and Instagram, this movement has blazed new and important ground about civic engagement and technology.

Healing Justice: Toward Transformative Organizing and Leadership

During the 2010 U.S. Social Forum in Detroit, nearly 300 organizers packed into Cobo Hall in the convention center to attend a workshop for organizers about a topic that deeply resonated with them, but few had actual language to describe. Eric Mann, director of the Strategy Center in Los Angeles, and N'gethe Maina, Director of Social Justice Leadership in New

York, eloquently codified the issue and provided a new way to think about organizing. N'gethe Maina opened with this statement:

> As we try and transform the structures and systems around people... the assumption is that, if you change the conditions around people, then that's going to allow people to change and to begin to lead good lives. But it is something of a gamble to believe that simply changing the conditions around any of us is going to remove the toxicity of oppression from inside us. (The Labor/ Community Strategy Center, 2015, para. 3)

Healing justice is not an entirely new idea. There are numerous leaders from past movements for justice who taught us that social change first begins with shifts in how we relate to others and treat the world. Cesar Chavez, Gandhi, Howard Thurman, Martin Luther King, Jr., and Malcolm X all taught us that social change is the result of deep healing and spiritual practice. Gandhi's satyagraha movement was rooted in using inner truth, love, and faith in order to transform oppressive economic and political systems.

Young social justice leaders are deploying the healing justice framework to transform schools and policies that harm young people. Similar to #Blacklivesmatter, youth leaders of color share the idea that it is important to develop an awareness of how toxic policies and structures influence their relationships, values, and behaviors. The broader healing justice movement to restore, resist, and reclaim is also present in young people's campaign to dismantle the willful defiance category of school misbehaviors in Los Angeles public schools. On May 14, 2013, the Los Angeles Unified School District (LAUSD) School Board voted to approve the School Climate Bill of Rights and roll back zero-tolerance discipline in all Los Angeles schools (Contractor & Staats, 2014). The decision was the result of organizing work of Brothers, Sons, Selves, a coalition of Los Angeles-based youth community organizations that developed the School Climate Bill of Rights, which outlines policies that promote student achievement and healthy school environments conducive to learning. The decision to adopt the School Climate Bill of Rights in LAUSD marked the first district in California to bar willful defiance as criteria for suspension (Contractor & Staats, 2014). Willful defiance is a rather vague category of behaviors ranging from dress code violations, refusing to complete classwork, to disrespecting a teacher. Researchers have found that willful defiance was largely responsible for disproportionate suspensions of African American and Latino students in urban districts like Los Angeles. These zero-tolerance practices gained momentum in the late 1990s (Skiba, 2000), in response to school shootings, and was rooted in the assumption that young people's behavior could be improved and modified by adopting zero tolerance for unwanted behaviors, which ultimately meant harsh punishment for violations of adult expectations of good behavior. Restorative justice represents an alternative to zero-tolerance policies that fueled and supported draconian discipline policies.

The district will employ restorative justice programs, which use peer support groups and group agreements to resolve conflicts between students, and students and teachers.

Young people, themselves the targets of these punitive policies, organized around implementing restorative practices rather than punishment in schools. Their campaign for restorative justice in Los Angeles is another example of how the healing justice movement shifts institutional and social values toward healing damaged relationships and community bonds. This organizing effort involved both changes in the harmful policy, and also shifts the relationship between the victim(s) and offender(s) in order to heal the harm. Repairing the harm often involves the offender accepting responsibility and agreeing to some form of restitution and/or compensation to the victim.

Restorative justice is an important strategy in the broader healing justice movement, particularly among communities of color. Not only do restorative justice strategies represent a fundamental shift in policies and practices in urban schools, they also provide important opportunities for young people and adults to prioritize healing and wellness, placing these values at the very center of classroom and school practices. Within school environments, restorative justice encourages administrators, teachers, and students to ask different questions. For example, rather than asking how might we stop fights at our school, a restorative approach might ask, "How might we increase and enhance peaceful interactions, and solutions among students, teachers, and the broader school environment?" Given the ways in which punishment-focused zero-tolerance policies have disproportionately harmed African American youth, and their communities, restorative justice strategies offer an important alternative to building peace, healing, and justice.

Conclusion

How do young activist leaders in Black communities respond to hopelessness in ways that restore human dignity, meaning, and possibility? How can these responses inform broader structural changes in civic, educational, and public safety? The healing justice movement offers one way to understand the unconventional, messy, and unclear path to justice.

Both #Blacklivesmatter and local efforts to dismantle zero-tolerance policies in schools illustrate how the fabric of justice is woven together by the brilliant strands of healing, love, and dignity. Together this fabric offers a mosaic of political possibilities that expand the confines of what constitutes civic and political. Leadership, in this sense, is much more like a love letter to justice than a prescriptive set of attributes. The love letter is vulnerable, honest, and imperfect, yet all the while striving, in all its might, to reach freedom and simply tell us how young people try to make the world a little better than it was when they arrived. Dr. Martin Luther King, Jr. (1968) in his speech, "Where Do We Go From Here" said,

> One of the great problems of history is that the concepts of love and power have usually been contrasted as opposites. What is needed is a realization that power without love is reckless and abusive, and that love without power is sentimental and anemic. Power at its best is love implementing the demands of justice, and justice at its best is power correcting everything that stands against love.

The new leadership of Black youth is fueled by majestic dignity and courageous love.

References

Benford, R., & Snow, D. (2000). Framing process and social movements: An overview and assessment. *Annual Review of Sociology, 26,* 611–639.

Center on Juvenile and Criminal Justice [CJCJ]. (1999). *Shattering "Broken Windows:" An analysis of San Francisco's alternative crime policies.* San Francisco, CA: Author.

Churchill, W., & Vander Wall, J. (2002). *The Cointellpro papers: Documents from the FBI.* Cambridge, MA: South End Press.

Contractor, D., & Staats, C. (2014). Interventions to address racialized discipline disparities and school "push out" (policy brief, 1-19). Columbus, OH: Kirwan Institute.

Coogler, R. (Director). (2013). *Fruitvale Station* [Motion picture]. United States: Forest Whitaker's Significant Productions.

Farmer, P. (2004). An anthropology of structural violence. *Current Anthropology, 45,* 305–325.

Garbarino, J. (1995). *Raising children in a socially toxic environment.* San Francisco, CA: Jossey-Bass.

Ginwright, S. (2010). *Black youth rising: Activism and radical healing in urban America.* New York, NY: Teachers College Press.

Goffman, E. (1974). *Frame analysis.* New York, NY: Harper Collins.

Jenkins, C. (1995). Social movements, political representation and the state: An agenda and comparative framework. In J. C. Jenkins & B. Klandermans (Eds.), *The politics of social protests: Comparative perspectives on states and social movements* (pp. 14–35). Minneapolis, MN: University of Minnesota Press.

King, M. L. (1968). *Where do we go from here: Chaos or community?* Boston, MA: Beacon Press.

Lee, N. (2014). *Healing-centered youth organizing: A framework for youth leadership in the 21st century.* Oakland, CA: Urban Peace Movement.

McAdam, D. (1982). *Political process and the development of Black insurgency, 1930–1970.* Chicago, IL: University of Chicago Press.

Morsillo, J., & Prilleltensky, I. (2007). Social action with youth: Interventions, evaluation, and psychopolitical validity. *Journal of Community Psychology, 35,* 725–740.

Padamsee, Y. M. (2011, June 19). Communities of care, organization for liberation [Web log post]. Retrieved from https://nayamaya.wordpress.com/category/community-care/

Piven, F., & Cloward, R. (1979). *Poor people's movements: Why they succeed, how they fail.* New York, NY: Vintage.

Prilleltensky, I., & Prilleltensky, O. (2006). *Promoting well-being: Linking personal, organizational, and community change.* Hoboken, NJ: Wiley.

Stelzer, A. (2015). #Blacklivesmatter: Alicia Garza on the origins of a movement. Retrieved from http://www.radioproject.org/2015/05/blacklivesmatter-alicia-garza-on-the-origins-of-a-movement/

Skiba, R. J. (2000). Zero tolerance, zero evidence: An analysis of school disciplinary practices. Bloomington, IN: Indiana Education Policy Center.

Snow, D., & Benford, R. (2000). Clarifying the relationship between framing and ideology in the study of social movements: A comment on Oliver and Johnston. *Mobilization, 5*, 55–60.

Snow, D. A., & Benford, R. D. (1988). Ideology, frame resonanace, and participant mobilization. *International Social Movements Research, 1*, 197–217.

The Labor/Community Strategy Center (2015). Transformative organizing theory workshop. Detroit, MI: U.S. Social Forum. Retrieved from http://www.thestrategycenter.org/transformative-organizing

Wallace, R. (2012). Healing justice workshop. Retrieved from http://www.crossroadsfund.org/blog/healingjustice

SHAWN A. GINWRIGHT is an associate professor of education in the Africana Studies Department and senior research associate for the Cesar Chavez Institute for Public Policy at San Francisco State University.

The authors trace the connections between multigenerational participatory action research and relational approaches to shared leadership, illustrating how the collective production of knowledge through research builds youth leadership capacity.

Leadership in Solidarity: Notions of Leadership Through Critical Participatory Action Research With Young People and Adults

Madeline Fox, Michelle Fine

A new Civil Rights Movement is happening outside our door, on our screens, and in our brunch spots (Rosenberg, 2015). In the United States, at the time of writing, many people are fed up with and fired up about institutionalized racism and especially racist police practices. The movement is unfolding in ways that were not part of social movements of the past, such as via social media (Evans, 2013). As events take place, national conversations can happen in the language of hashtags: #Blacklivesmatter; #wecantbreathe; #thisstopstoday. In this age of social media, where conversations can be immediately participatory, across geographies, in real-time and in ever-evolving ways, one of the important characteristics of the #Blacklivesmatter movement is that there is no singular charismatic leader. It was collectively launched by Alicia Garza, Opal Tometi, and Patrisse Cullors and taken up, carried forward by a network of organizers and activists. Oprah Winfrey criticized this "leaderlessness," calling it a weakness, and yet (and as the Twitterverse quickly responded) many tout the diffused leadership style of the #Blacklivesmatter movement as central to its energy and effectiveness (Somashekhar, 2015).

Taking inspiration from the #Blacklivesmatter movement, in this chapter we reflect on how critical participatory action research can provide insight into the kind of leadership we need to cultivate in our movements, our classrooms, our research, and our lives. We have found in our own research that a participatory approach, emphasizing collectivity and shared

NEW DIRECTIONS FOR STUDENT LEADERSHIP, no. 148, Winter 2015 © 2015 Wiley Periodicals, Inc., A Wiley Company
Published online in Wiley Online Library (wileyonlinelibrary.com) • DOI: 10.1002/yd.20152

45

expertise, produces rigorous and politically powerful results. In other words, how we go about conducting research, and who gets included as knowledge producers, matters. This is a key insight for leadership development rather than the development of individual leaders for social change.

The chapter begins with a theoretical framing of leadership in the context of participatory research; we then provide a background on participatory action research as epistemology and approach, including a detailed description of the Polling for Justice research project. Finally, using the Polling for Justice study to illustrate, we articulate three notions of leadership from participatory action research praxis: expertise as shared, cultivating a critical lens, and relational methodologies toward building movements.

A Collectivist Relational Approach: Group-Centered Leadership

In this chapter, we use Ella Jo Baker's group-centered leadership model (Cohen, Jackson, & London, 2014) as the frame to understand and aspire to leadership for knowledge production and social change. Baker, a central leader of the Black Freedom movement, believed that change takes place from the bottom up. She practiced a group-centered leadership style (Ransby, 2003) despite the national attention and rewards given to the more charismatic leaders of the Civil Rights movement. "Baker's message was that oppressed people, whatever their level of formal education, had the ability to understand and interpret the world around them, to see that world for what it was and to move to transform it" (Ransby, 2003, p. 7). Baker believed those most impacted had to be the ones to take action. Baker's radical ideas on leadership are rooted in her theoretical understanding of oppression; she considered all of us as interconnected and interdependent, " ... the poor and afflicted ... were not some reified and depraved 'other,' but rather an extension of self ... " (Ransby, 2003, p. 11).

Further, we use a relational model of leadership, meaning that we are not considering leadership as a set of characteristics or attributes of an individual, but rather as a dynamic system, a set of processes, out of which moments of leadership occur (Uhl-Bien, 2006). Leadership can, therefore, be understood much in the way that Foucault (1977) describes the distributed nature of power. From this lens, leadership takes place in various ways within a group and is not limited to the most visible voice or person. In a multiyear study on leadership within social change organizations using a relational leadership model, Sonia Ospina and colleagues (2012) found that leadership can be understood as praxis. In their findings, reframing discourse, bridging difference, and unleashing human energies were the key effective types of leadership work taking place in social change organizations (Ospina et al., 2012, p. xl; p. 268). Likewise, in this chapter, we take up a group-centered, relational leadership approach within multigenerational critical participatory action research projects. We believe participatory action research approaches provide a praxis through which to achieve and develop collectivist, relational, group-centered leadership. Through a focus on multigenerational research, we explore how revolutionizing approaches to leadership within research can contribute to social transformation and liberation.

Multigenerational Critical Participatory Action Research

Adult–youth relationships are defined by power. You can hear and see this quite literally in the actual furniture of multigenerational spaces, and the language of our interactions. Youth chairs face a teacher's desk in a classroom; young people are often spoken to as if they need correcting; and teenagers are derided for being too irresponsible, too impulsive, too easily influenced by peers, and too concerned with their own bodies (Lesko, 2001). Although adolescence is a time marked by an increase in independence, it is also a group defined in part by an absence of power (Bakan, 1971; Lesko, 2001).

As a society, conceptions of adolescence are produced as a technology for social control (Lesko, 2001). In other words, through schooling, parenting, popular media, and beyond, society makes use of adolescents to shape what citizenship means, what American means, what a good adult, good man, good woman means, and what criminal means. We need more spaces and opportunities to develop critical leadership grounded in a justice frame—and in this chapter, we propose that critical participatory action research with young people provides a praxis for this work.

Participatory Action Research.   Participatory action research (PAR) is an epistemological approach and ethical commitment that positions those considered the subject of research as the researchers themselves. In PAR, those impacted by an area of inquiry come together as a research collective, along with allies including academics or community workers, to define for themselves the research question, create a research design, collect data, analyze data, and decide together what should be done with the results. In this way, participation in knowledge production is opened to those traditionally excluded from being knowledge producers within the academy and beyond. Popular education approaches of Paolo Freire, the liberation psychology of Ignacio Martín Baró, the action research of Kurt Lewin, the critical social science of W. E. B. DuBois, and critical theory are all theoretical traditions informing PAR, a method shaped over time by a broad range of scholars, educators, and activists carefully considering questions of who has access to knowledge production (Friere, 1970; Hart et al., 1997; Lykes & Mallona, 2008; Tuck, 2009).

In this chapter, we build on the body of work produced by the Public Science Project (Fine, 2015) at The Graduate Center of the City of the University of New York. The Public Science Project is an incubator for participatory action research projects where we conduct critical participatory action research. We use *critical* to signal a commitment to feminist, queer, critical race, indigenous, and neo-Marxist theories (Torre, Cahill, & Fox, 2015), and thus in our projects, we map the ways power is intertwined with knowledge. We interrogate the relationships between everyday individual experiences, social structures, history, and injustice (Torre, Fine, Stoudt, & Fox, 2012). As part of this critical stance, when investigating youth experiences and expertise, we adopt a critical youth studies frame (James & James, 2001; Jenks, 1996).

In line with this critical commitment, and in recognition of the ways power is infused in adult–youth relationships, we tend not to describe our PAR projects with young people as youth participatory action research, or YPAR. In our research projects on adolescence, young people and adults join together with the idea that through pooling differently positioned expertise, what some have called *situated knowledges* (Harding, 1995), we strengthen the research we produce. We describe research collectives as multigenerational PAR to make explicit that we value the expertise of each group member, from young people to adult members.

In order to include youth and adults together across race/ethnicity, class, gender, sexuality, immigration status, and ability, and to be a multigenerational research team, we pay careful attention to the construction of the research space and our everyday praxis. Our research spaces are designed to foster collaboration across difference, out of a belief that to make sense of injustice we need to recognize ways we are mutually implicated in each other's messy lives. We are committed to building multigenerational research collectives producing knowledge collectively and harvesting various forms of situated expertise to generate new understandings and enactments of adolescence.

Doing PAR with young people nurtures leadership, and in particular, relational leadership rooted in collectivity. The commitments of critical PAR lead us to adopt a collective model of shared leadership.

Critical PAR and Polling for Justice

The Polling for Justice study was conducted over 3 years between 2008 and 2011 in New York City out of the Public Science Project of the CUNY Graduate Center. The study was conceived as a multigenerational research project, and it grew out of a collective desire from youth-centered community organizations and the Public Science Project to document current conditions for the City's youth. The project included over 40 young people from across New York City along with academics, community organizers, public health officials, and community-based lawyers. The heart of the study was a city-wide youth-to-youth survey that focused on youth experiences at the intersections of education, public health, criminal justice, and community safety. We, the Polling for Justice research team, surveyed young people, ages 14–21 across New York City and also conducted several data-driven focus groups with key groups of underrepresented young people.

The Polling for Justice Project's survey was designed, over the course of 6 months, by a research team of academic faculty, graduate students, and diverse high school and college-age youth, with periodic input from lawyers, public-health researchers, artists, and community activists. After scouring standardized instruments on youth experiences of school, health, and criminal justice, and spending time developing "home grown" items, we produced a survey protocol that was distributed on the streets and online, to a sample of 1,100.

Although the Polling for Justice (PFJ) study has been analyzed elsewhere (Fine, Stoudt, Fox, & Santos, 2010; Stoudt, Fox, & Fine, 2012), in this chapter, the focus is on the research process for building leadership through critical inquiry and the power to frame youth problems as structural inequities. Below we provide a brief overview of the findings and scope of the study.

Polling for Justice Findings. In the PFJ survey we asked questions about youth experiences with schooling, public health, policing, and the criminal justice system. Additional survey questions focused on home and family life. The survey findings revealed a set of positive results in relation to aspirations, community engagement, and schooling: Most survey respondents reported having high educational aspirations and feeling hopeful about the future. Young people reported caring about working with other young people to improve their communities and in some ways feeling good about parts of their schooling experience. On these measures, there were basically no racial/ethnic, gender, or geographic differences—it was all good news.

Young people also reported uneven access to health care and health education, and dissatisfaction with their schooling experiences: Survey respondents reported that in their school students act rudely toward teachers in their classes, feel bored, believe that too much class time is spent getting ready to pass high-stakes standardized tests, and report overcrowded classrooms. The survey results revealed that students feel that school rules, tests, and the way personnel treat students made them feel pushed to leave school. In addition, we heard about young people's everyday, normalized experiences with police, which are described in more detail below.

Our analysis brought us to an understanding of the spread and speed by which injustice experiences for young people carry across interdependent circuits. In other words, not just "bad things happen to poor kids" but policies differentially affect (and connect) young people and adults, rich and poor, across race/ethnicity, geography, gender, sexuality, and privilege, with highly uneven frequency and consequences. Wealthy children found with drugs in school may have a parent or psychiatrist called, rarely a police officer; it is not the same for low-income students, who have the "luxury" of police stationed in their schools, ready for the arrest. The loss of resources, human rights, dignity, legitimacy, and opportunities in one community corresponds with their respective accumulation in another. We call these dynamics "circuits of ... dispossession" and privilege (Fine & Ruglis, 2009, p. 20).

Further, we found serious and uneven collateral consequences for youth experiencing cross-sector policy dispossession. Young people who have had at least one negative experience in each of the four policy sectors analyzed in our study (education, criminal justice, public health, and home and family life) were more likely to also have reported more feelings of depression and/or to have put themselves in harm's way in terms of risky sexual behavior, violent situations, drugs, and alcohol.

Although the survey revealed a number of troubling trends faced by New York City youth, our focus here is how the research itself helped provide channels for leadership education. Throughout the process of research, each member of the PFJ research collective contributed meaningfully to the whole. The critical participatory action research praxis, rooted in collectivity, provides a frame through which to consider leadership, leader development, and leadership development. (See Chapter 1.)

Notions on Leadership From PAR.   The experience of engaging in participatory action research as the Polling for Justice research collective was an exercise in developing-through-doing, a relational, collectivist group-centered leadership style. What follows are three strategic commitments of critical PAR we believe facilitated leadership (with and for) in the Polling for Justice multigenerational participatory action research process.

Notion One: Expertise Is Shared. Our research design, analyses, and products are generated from the expertise of those who have most often been excluded from traditional research—in this case, young people of color from low-income areas of New York City. Central to a participatory action research approach is the recognition that knowledge and expertise come in many forms; situated knowledge is born in distinct soil. And the knowledge that grows from oppression is particularly significant for shaping research projects to be of use in community struggles (Fine & Barrerras, 2001). We recognize that marginalized youth have been denied what Appadurai (2006) calls "the right to research" (p. 168), and that low-income communities and youth in particular should be respected with the ethic, "no research on us without us."

In the multigenerational research team that made up the PFJ project, we each contributed meaningfully toward producing knowledge collectively. For some of the young people, their expertise came from everyday experiences with the topics in which we were interested, like schooling, criminal justice, and public health. For some of the adults, their expertise came from their backgrounds as scholars, educators, community lawyers, and/or public health advocates. It strengthened the survey questions to take into account informed adult ideas and critical knowledge of historical trends, context, and past research. The collective highly valued the particular expertise of the everyday that young people contributed. The most politically powerful parts of our survey were the questions crafted by the youth researchers, grown from their experiences and expertise.

The most vivid instances of these questions were those related to the criminal justice system. The small group of youth and adult researchers who developed survey questions in this area started by examining existing surveys and literature for standardized questions to include in the PFJ survey. However, over 2 days of searching, they found very little that reflected their own ideas of what might be important to ask. The young people were especially frustrated with the questions they found from existing surveys on youth experiences with criminal justice. Many of the survey questions they found were worded from the perspective of adults and riddled with assumptions about youth as suspect, criminal, and violent. For example, one survey asked the question: "If a kid carried a gun in your neighborhood, would he/she be caught by the police?" (Arizona Criminal Justice Commission, 2006). The questions presumed that young people were fist-fighting, gang-belonging, and/or gun-carrying (Arizona Criminal Justice Commission, 2006; Gotbaum, 2008). They echoed all-too-familiar representations of youth that the Polling for Justice research team wanted to reject or at least complicate. Deciding that the language from pre-existing questions was at best inadequate, and privileging the young people's lived experiences as expertise, they crafted a detailed matrix on intimate and everyday experiences with police seen in Figure 4.1.

This set of questions ended up producing some of our most powerful findings. Young people reported alarmingly high levels of negative interactions with the police. The findings described especially high levels of negative interactions with police experienced by LGBTQ young people. In

Figure 4.1.   PFJ Survey Questions on Daily Youth Interactions
With Police

About You and the Criminal Justice System			
In the past 6 months, haveany of the following happened to you?			
	Never	Yes, happened out of school	Yes happened in school
I was told to move by the police in a disrespectful way.	☐	☐	☐
I was arrested.	☐	☐	☐
I was helped by a police officer.	☐	☐	☐
I got a ticket/summons.	☐	☐	☐
I was given a"second chance" by a police officer.	☐	☐	☐
I was picked up for a PINS (person in need of supervision) violation.	☐	☐	☐
I was stopped by the police for questioning.	☐	☐	☐
I was frisked (patted-down).	☐	☐	☐
I was stripped searched.	☐	☐	☐
A police officer crossed the line(touched in appropriately) while searching me.	☐	☐	☐
I received "sexual attention" from the police.	☐	☐	☐
I was threatened and/or called a name by the police.	☐	☐	☐

addition, we found that negative experiences are accumulated most by young men, young people of color, and young people from low-income areas.

Through these experiences, the PAR overlapped with our understanding of leadership development. Our commitment to valuing various types of expertise not only cultivated each young person's idea of themselves as a meaningful contributor, but also provided the scaffold necessary to allow each group member to contribute new ideas. The commitment to expertise as shared made room for young people, traditionally excluded from knowledge production, to contribute important new questions on young people's daily experiences with police, and as a result, the PFJ study as a whole was able to contribute meaningfully to the field—in other words, to lead with their expertise.

Notion Two: Cultivating a Critical Lens. The commitment to developing a critical lens is a key ingredient in PAR projects. The invitation to be critical, to question, and to consider context is an invitation to rethink the world around us. In critical PAR, in order to make collective sense of the world we live in, we work together to cultivate critical understandings of history, context, and current experiences. During what we call a *research camp*, prior to developing our research questions or instruments, we build a collective infrastructure for gathering and pooling our various knowledges, and our ignorances; what we know, what we don't know, and what we don't even know we don't know. This can include reading articles together, listening to music, writing creatively from a shared video clip, developing a historical analysis of root causes of lives, reading and digesting critical theory, and seeing individual experiences as shared. As we work, we are carefully interrogating, transforming, questioning, and reimagining new theories as we go. This process may be considered a remix of history, folklore, experience, research methods, and critical reclaiming of a public science. In Public Science Project research collectives, we develop a praxis of leadership rooted in our critical stance, centered around collective goals, and designed for each individual to contribute to the whole.

In PFJ, we learned the history of how public institutions and policies of education, criminal justice, and public health were constructed. We learned and practiced critical theory, always considering power and voices, perspectives, and experiences we might be occluding or overlooking. And we turned to our individual life stories and experiences, in addition to the data-in-aggregate from the survey. Iterating back and forth between life stories and survey data, we learned unequivocally that gender, race, ethnicity, sexuality, probably skin color, and definitely neighborhood, matter in terms of cumulative experiences of dispossession.

We documented from our own data that young people who have been legally, verbally, physically, and/or sexually assaulted by a police officer report higher levels of psychological struggle than those who have not (Fine et al., 2010).

Figure 4.2.   PFJ Survey Data on Daily Youth Interactions With Police

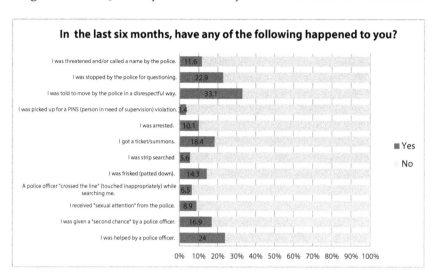

When mapped, in Figure 4.2, the data made evident that certain neighborhoods and populations bore the brunt of aggressive policing: young people from central Brooklyn and south Bronx, youth of color more than White youth, and males more than females reported the highest levels of negative interactions with police. We learned that young people who identified as lesbian, gay, bisexual, or questioning reported alarmingly high levels of negative interactions with police, as seen in Figure 4.3.

Meanwhile, the PFJ research collective members were sharing our own stories of interactions with police. Some of us had arrest stories, many had harassment stories, we all had witness stories, and others shared their desire to become police officers themselves. The work of understanding the data from the survey helped us see how our individual experiences were shared and we made note of patterns and disjuncture. In general, the experiences PFJ youth researchers shared within our research collective helped us to understand how experiences of policing are normalized for young people in New York City. Our life stories in juxtaposition with survey data led us to theorize that in order to interrupt this normalization, we need to shift our understanding of youth experiences of policing and other dispossessing experiences as a societal/public issue located somewhere in the space between youth and adults.

Our survey data alongside the collective personal experiences of our group provoked a layered, structural, and critical analysis about race, community, sexuality, and policing that certainly would not have been possible had we been thinking in isolation or simply as White adult academics

Figure 4.3.   Negative Police Contact Reported by Sexuality

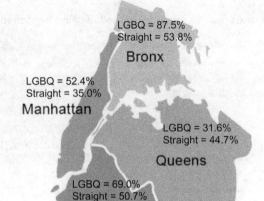

living far from communities characterized by high rates of aggressive policing, school closings, and stop-and-frisk activities.

The critical lens we cultivated within the research team made evident the ways that our experiences are inflected by power and privilege but also bound up in one another. Powell Pruitt (2004) retheorizes the achievement gap, proposing instead we consider it an achievement knot in order to take into account the ways we are all implicated by, and responsible for, the educational experiences of youth of color. In other words, developing an understanding of how our everyday experiences were historically and sociopolitically constructed was crucial for constructing a space where we invited new ways of being, new adult–youth relations, and space for new expressions of leadership.

Notion three. Participatory Relational Methodologies Toward Building a Movement. In order to share expertise across generations and cultivate a critical lens, it is necessary to craft the conditions in which PAR can take place across generation and positionality carefully. In our PAR spaces, we take great care to establish the research space as a radical alternative to the top-down leadership structure of traditional classrooms and research labs (Torre & Fine, 2004).

Motivated by big ideas, the work often comes down to small details. To establish a radically alternative space for very differentially positioned youth and adults to think together, produce knowledge together, and lead together, it is necessary to consider the arrangement of the room, time of the meetings, the food being served, the compensation provided, how people's fantasies of science, expertise, and risk haunt the room, and the scaffolding of the work itself.

The adult role of PFJ Project Director (held by Maddy Fox) was enacted in the manner of project organizer. That is, Fox took on the work of setting the space in which the process of collective sense-making could take place. This included a wide range of tasks and work, from the mundane (room reservations, passport applications, and flight reservations; video recorders, tape recorders, journals, pens, and markers; pizza orders, snack runs, time-sheets, and computer passwords and home-grown youth-researcher IDs) to the substantive (creating the structure for each session, in collaboration with others, through which we did the work). We considered these more routine tasks crucial to making the content of the work possible. For the more substantive aspects of the research work—analyzing survey and fo-cus group data—youth and adults cofacilitated a research process toward our collective project goals. Our research meeting agendas were cocon-structed and collaboratively carried out by the multigenerational research team.

In PFJ, we knew that the more we had ritualized set routines for each meeting, the more the group would feel/behave like a collective instead of a more conventional top-down classroom. With shared knowledge about what was going to happen next, leadership could also be shared. Each meet-ing began with a check-in—a time for each person to say how he or she was doing that particular week before we launched into whatever the work was that day. The experiences we told each other echoed the disturbing racial-ized, classed, and sexualized patterns of dispossession emerging from our survey analyses. Although at first we conceived the check-ins as part of the scaffolding of our group, but ancillary to our research, we eventually came to see how the events of our daily lives mirrored and complicated the data we were analyzing from the survey.

This swapping of life stories within the context of a participatory action research collective was a form of critical bifocality, by which we mean the in-terrogation of clear evidence of structural violence and injustice, with the si-multaneous embodied evidence of agency, resistance, contestation, despair, hope, and desire in motion (Weis & Fine, 2012). As part of this multigen-erational participatory praxis, by providing opportunity to share intimately with each other across generations we built complex relationships with each other. These relationships allowed each member to take on varied roles in our group, including leadership roles. Leadership was shared, moment-by-moment, but also in terms of the whole. The PFJ collective carefully con-structed a felt sense of shared leadership.

Believing leadership to be a process, there was room for each of us to step into leadership at different moments, in different ways. We used artistic-embodied methodologies, like Playback Theatre and other improvisational theater methods, to put the survey and focus group findings up on their feet (Fox, 2014). We found this methodology was effective at facilitating our group to theorize together and work as a collective—without privileging certain experiences, like agility with statistics or writing. Artistic embodied methodologies provided a praxis for enacting group-centered leadership in the context of data analysis and participatory knowledge production. As we would work together to make a human sculpture or a scene out of a set of cross-tabulations from our survey, the person who had the strongest relationship to that piece of data, or whoever was struck with a creative idea, would lead the work.

Conclusion

The findings from the PFJ project circulated in multiple ways. We contributed to scholarship articles and chapters, we performed our research in provocative participatory performances, and at various points the findings from the study fed youth-centered organizing campaigns: to end mayoral control of the public education system, and to reform policing inside and outside of schools. Most significantly, several research projects based out of the Public Science Project at the CUNY Graduate Center picked up where PFJ left off, including two studies on policing and community safety: the Morris Justice Project and Researchers for Fair Policing; and a study looking at the school discipline experiences for high school students identifying as LGBTQ.

In these ways, the work of producing knowledge collectively, across generations, and centered on youth experiences was an instance of leadership in motion. Through a participatory action research approach, we enact leadership as shared, relational, and group centered. With commitments to shared expertise, critical perspectives, and participatory relational methodologies, multigenerational critical PAR research collectives not only contribute a praxis for youth (and adult) leadership, but the leadership enacted contributes to knowledge production, policy reform, reimagined adult–youth relations, and liberation.

The story of the #Blacklivesmatter movement, as it continues to unfold, reinforces the urgent need we have for spaces to practice radical forms of leadership, group-centered rather than "expertly" led. Through a critical participatory action research approach, with multigenerational research collectives, we can produce scholarship—rigorous scholarship with relevance in our communities. In the process, through broadening our definitions of expertise, learning and applying critical theory, and paying attention to participatory methodologies at every stage and at every level of the process, we can practice group-centered leadership, replacing the diminished power of adolescence with reimagined adult–youth relationships and a mighty strength in numbers.

References

Appadurai, A. (2006). The right to research. *Globalisation, societies and education, 4*(2), 167–177. doi:10.1080/14767720600750696

Arizona Criminal Justice Commission. (2006). *Arizona youth survey instrument.* Retrieved from http://www.azcjc.gov/ACJC.Web/sac/AYSReports/2008/2006_Arizona_Youth_Survey_Instrument.pdf

Bakan, D. (1971). Adolescence in America: From idea to social fact. *Daedalus, 100,* 979–995.

Cohen, C., Jackson, E., & London, M. (2014). *Black youth project.* Presented at the Research to Performance Symposium of the American Educational Researcher Association, Chicago, IL.

Evans, M. (2013). Mapping social media networks in youth organizing. *Journal of Information, Information Technology, and Organizations, 8,* 67–82.

Fine, M. (2015). Global provocations: Critical reflections on community based research and intervention designed at the intersections of global dynamics and local cultures. *Community Psychology in Global Perspective, 1*(1), 5–15.

Fine, M., & Barreras, R. (2001). To be of use. *Analyses of Social Issues and Public Policy, 1*(1), 175–182. doi:10.1111/1530–2415.00012

Fine, M., & Ruglis, J. (2009). Circuits and consequences of dispossession: The racialized realignment of the public sphere for U.S. youth. *Transforming Anthropology, 17*(1), 20–33. doi:10.1111/j.1548–7466.2009.01037.x

Fine, M., Stoudt, B., Fox, M., & Santos, M. (2010, September). The uneven distribution of social suffering: Documenting the social health consequences of neo-liberal social policy on marginalized youth. *European Health Psychologist, 12,* 30–35.

Foucault, M. (1977). *Discipline and punish: The birth of the prison.* New York, NY: Vintage.

Fox, M. (2014). The knowing body: Participatory artistic embodied methodologies for re-imagining adolescence. *Dissertations and Theses, 2014–Present.* Paper 210.

Friere, P. (1970). Cultural action and conscientization. *Harvard Educational Review, 40*(3), 452–477.

Gotbaum, B. (2008). Old problem new eyes: Youth insights on gangs in New York City. Office of the Public Advocate of the City of New York. Retrieved from: http://publicadvocategotbaum.com/policy/documents/gangs-recs-comboreportfinal.pdf.

Harding, S. (1995). "Strong objectivity:" A response to the new objectivity question. *Synthese, 104,* 331–349. doi:10.1007/BF01064504

Hart, R., Daiute, C., Iltus, S., Kritt, D., Rome, M., & Sabo, K. (1997). Developmental theory and children's participation in community organizations. *Social Justice, 24*(3), 33–63.

James, A., & James, A. (2001). Childhood: Toward a theory of continuity and change. *Annals of the American Academy of Political and Social Science, 575*(1), 25–37.

Jenks, C. (1996). *Childhood.* New York, NY: Routledge.

Lesko, N. (2001). Act your age!: A cultural construction of adolescence. New York, NY: Routledge.

Lykes, M. B., & Mallona, A. (2008). Towards transformational liberation: Participatory and action research and praxis. In P. Reason & H. Bradbury (Eds.), *The Sage handbook of action research: Participative inquiry and practice* (pp. 106–120). London, England: Sage.

Ospina, S., Foldy, E. G., El Hadidy, W., Dodge, J., Hofmann-Pinilla, A., & Su, C. (2012). Social change leadership as relational leadership. In M. Uhl-Bien & S. Ospina (Eds.), *Advancing relational leadership research: A dialogue among perspectives* (pp. 255–302). Charlotte, NC: Information Age Publishing.

Powell Pruitt, L. (2004). The achievement (k)not: Whiteness and "Black underachievement." In Michelle Fine (Ed.), *Off white: Readings on power, privilege, and resistance* (2nd ed., pp. 235–244). New York, NY: Routledge.

Ransby, B. (2003). *Ella Baker and the Black freedom movement: A radical democratic vision.* Chapel Hill, NC: University of North Carolina Press.

Rosenberg, E. (2015, January 5). Protesters storm brunch joints to protest police brutality. New York Daily News. Retrieved from http://nydn.us/11eDl6k

Somashekhar, S. (2015, January 6). Oprah says protesters lack clear demands. Here's what they do want. *The Washington Post.* Retrieved from http://www.washingtonpost.com/news/post-nation/wp/2015/01/06/oprah-says-protesters-lack-clear-demands-heres-what-they-do-want/

Stoudt, B., Fox, M., & Fine, M. (2012). Contesting privilege with critical participatory action research. *Journal of Social Issues, 68*(1), 178–193. doi:10.1111/j.1540-4560.2011.01743.x

Torre, M. E., Cahill, C., & Fox, M. (2015). Participatory action research in social research. In J. D. Wright (editor-in-chief), *International encyclopedia of the social & behavioral sciences* (2nd ed., Vol. 17, pp. 540–544). Oxford, England: Elsevier.

Torre, M. E., & Fine, M. (2004). Re-membering exclusions: Participatory action research in public institutions. *Qualitative Research in Psychology, 1*(1), 15–37. doi:10.1191/1478088704qp003oa

Torre, M. E., Fine, M., Stoudt, B. G., & Fox, M. (2012). Critical participatory action research as public science. In H. Cooper, P. M. Camic, D. L. Long, A. T. Panter, D. Rindskopf, & K. J. Sher (Eds.), *APA handbook of research methods in psychology, Research designs: Quantitative, qualitative, neuropsychological, and biological* (Vol. 2, pp. 171–184). Washington, DC: American Psychological Association. Retrieved from http://content.apa.org/books/13620--011

Tuck, E. (2009). Re-visioning action: Participatory action research and indigenous theories of change. *The Urban Review, 41*(1), 47–65. doi:10.1007/s11256–008–0094-x

Uhl-Bien, M. (2006). Relational leadership theory: Exploring the social processes of leadership and organizing. *The Leadership Quarterly, 17,* 654–676. doi:10.1016/j.leaqua.2006.10.007

Weis, L., & Fine, M. (2012). Critical bifocality and circuits of privilege: Expanding critical ethnographic theory and design. *Harvard Educational Review, 82*(2), 173–201.

MADELINE FOX *is assistant professor of children and youth studies and sociology at Brooklyn College.*

MICHELLE FINE *is distinguished professor, psychology, at City University of New York Graduate Center.*

5

Diverse urban youth need a wide range of program opportunities and formats to develop their own sense of political agency and leadership. One size does not fit all.

Summer in the City: Cultivating Political Agents in Boston Out-of-School-Time Programs

Felicia M. Sullivan

It's Summer 2011. Boston's neighborhoods are alive with thousands of teens involved in programs ranging from academic enrichment to sports camps to summer jobs. At a community park in Dorchester, Taylor is finishing the construction of a raised garden bed for community members to grow vegetables. Her new friend, Eva, is at the edge of the park handing out fliers inviting residents to an evening of fun activities. Meanwhile, Jae and JD are cutting back a patch of invasive Japanese knotweed—a park conservation effort. They will meet up with others later to prepare for community night festivities. This summer jobs program is part of the Friends of Beardsley Park Youth Park Stewards' program (all organizational and student names in this chapter are pseudonyms, with the exception of the Castle Square Tenants Organization).

In the South End, a few neighborhoods away, Melinda is painting an office in the community center at Castle Square Apartments. The office will double as space for an early childhood program. Down the hall, Stephanie is supporting a group of young children in an art project. Elsewhere, BD is helping his friend Ben with dance moves. Both will soon be performing at a community night event in the neighborhood. These teens belong to the Teen Center, one of the many constituent programs run by the Castle Square Tenants Organization.

In Roxbury, Hector and Natalie are going door-to-door in the Mission Hill area asking residents to fill out a community needs survey. Their organizing teammates Karen and Javier are back at the center. Karen is working with program staff to plan the next youth organizing meeting as part of her

New Directions for Student Leadership, no. 148, Winter 2015 © 2015 Wiley Periodicals, Inc., A Wiley Company
Published online in Wiley Online Library (wileyonlinelibrary.com) • DOI: 10.1002/yd.20153

teen leadership position. Javier is chilling in the music room before getting started on his own door-to-door knocking tasks. These teens are all members of the Centro Cultural Latino's Community Organizers.

At a high school sitting between Dorchester and Jamaica Plain, Simone is conferring with other members on her leadership team to see how the day's educational seminars are going for the summer Youth Lead program. She is a returning member of the program offered by the State Street Institute. Later she will be prepping materials for a community education workshop on the school-to-prison pipeline, which she and another teen will conduct for a community group in Roxbury.

These teens attend Boston Public Schools (BPS), from competitive exam schools like Boston Latin Academy to pilots like the Boston Community Leadership Academy to vocational schools like Madison Park. They are demographically similar to other students in the BPS system. They live in many neighborhoods—Dorchester, Roxbury's Mission Hill, South End, West End, East Boston, Jamaica Plain, Mattapan, and Downtown—in families with low to moderate incomes. A handful are more solidly middle class. Single-parent or guardian households that are non-English speaking with at least one foreign-born guardian are common. These young people mirror the demographics of the organizations in which they are engaged.

In these diverse settings, the teens are developing leadership capacities with a decidedly political bent. They strengthen their individual voice and self-efficacy, gain the ability to work with others to achieve individual and collective goals, and improve their understanding of public issues and the means to act positively upon them. As in programs that seek youth leadership development without political aims, these teens grow their individual skills, identities, and capacities while learning what it is to act responsibly in a civic arena and appreciate differences (Bresso, 2012; Cress, Astin, Zimmerman-Oster, & Burkhardt, 2001). They build connections and relationships, and often serve the needs of the community at-large as experts of their own experience (Clyde, 2010; Roberts, 2007; Wheeler & Edlebeck, 2006).

Out-of-School Time in Boston

These Boston teens are fortunate to have multiple sectors, including a robust non-profit sector, working to address their needs and interests. With over 5,000 organizations, Boston's nonprofit sector is diverse, with small grassroots groups and large economic engines such as nationally recognized hospitals and universities (Keating, Pradhan, Wasall, & DeNatale, 2008). Approximately 5% are oriented toward youth development, sports, and recreation (Massachusetts Nonprofit Database, 2010), but one can find youth-serving programs in a much wider range of organizations. Community action agencies (e.g., Action for Boston Community Development) and community development corporations (e.g. Dorchester Bay Economic

Table 5.1   Case Study Organizations and Program Sites

Organization/Program (Neighborhood)	Mission
Castle Square Tenants Organization/Teen Center (South End)	Works to maintain affordable housing in the community and is a strong advocate of programs and services needed to build vibrant and safe communities.
Friends of Beardsley Park/Youth Park Stewards (Dorchester/Jamaica Plain)	Seeks to restore and preserve Beardsley Park, a historic urban green space located in the geographic heart of Boston.
Centro Cultural Latino/Community Organizers (Mission Hill in Roxbury)	Works in partnership with Latino youth and families to end destructive cycles of poverty, health disparities, and lack of opportunity in their community.
State Street Institute/Youth Lead (Dorchester)	Develops and strengthens the power of youth to work toward building a just society.

Note: All organizations and programs are pseudonyms except for the Castle Square Tenants Organization.

Development Corporation) offer programs targeted toward young residents as part of community revitalization efforts. Arts organizations (e.g., the writer's group Grub Street, the arts and crafts Elliot School) serve a general population with youth as one constituency. Still other nonprofits like Project Hope, Episcopal City Mission, and Codman Square Health Center meet a range of social, health, and educational needs of youth either directly or indirectly as part of comprehensive family support.

The 13 young people described above participate in four summer programs in Boston's opportunity-rich out-of-school-time environment (see Table 5.1) and provide a small window into the larger population of nonprofit out-of-school-time programs available to Boston youth. The programs selected for this study are offered in the City of Boston by formal 501c3 nonprofit organizations incorporated in the city. These organizations identify as human service (the city's largest nonprofit service area), have budgets of at least $100K and under $1M, and serve teens either exclusively or as part of a larger constituency base. This multicase study looked at three different units of analysis—youth, programs, and organizations—in order to understand the learning contexts that promote political agency and civic leadership.

Political Efficacy, Sociopolitical Development, and Civic Leadership

To promote civic and political leadership, out-of-school-time programs ideally should help their young members understand how to make decisions about public issues as well as create a vision for a better society (Bresso, 2012; Giroux, 2005). Youth leadership is an important outcome of youth development processes (Kress, 2006). To do this, youth first need to believe that they have the capacity to act for themselves and for others. This capacity, internal political efficacy, is traditionally composed of four separate elements (Morrell, 2003):

1. Ability to understand or have knowledge of political or community issues
2. Feeling able to participate in political or community issues
3. Feeling well informed about issues being discussed
4. Feeling as equipped as others to make decisions

During 1-hour, semistructured interviews in 2011 and early 2012, the teens in this study were asked what they thought about their ability and confidence in affecting change and making decisions—key markers of civic and political leadership. Specifically, they were asked:

What do you think is the most important issue facing you as a young person?

What would you do to start working toward addressing this issue?

Their transcribed responses were coded against the four internal political efficacy indicators. All of the teens identified at least one important issue and understood or had core knowledge of that issue. Often these issues related to personal experiences (e.g., violence, health behaviors, interpersonal relationships). Almost all teens felt they could act to make change or felt equipped to make decisions. Many could talk about their issue with authority and confidence in a detailed manner. Many were also able to propose specific actions to address the issue. For example, when asked what he would change, JD at the Youth Park Stewards shared:

Yeah, I mean there's a lot of things that could be changed but I just want to ... change more people using their resources, and using other things that are not necessary, like building new buildings and stuff ... Like, instead of building a track field, and a football field, you could just go to Beardsley Park, and there's like ... a ton of grass, and you could run everywhere. Like they do track races and stuff ... Yeah, they just waste money, and it sucks. Like, if you saved all that money from however many football fields, and baseball fields and track fields they did ... and just came to the park and ran ... we'd have a lot of money left over (personal communication, August 10, 2011)

Not all teens could articulate a plan or conceive of how they might begin to act. For instance, Taylor, also at the Youth Park Stewards, when asked how she would begin to make change on her issue said, "I don't even know, to be honest with you" (personal communication, August 10, 2011).

Because indicators of internal political efficacy were consistent across the teens in all programs, it could be argued that this is simply adolescent development. The teens were in a close age cohort ranging from 14 to 18 years, averaging 16 years, and political knowledge increases from age 14 to later teen years (Torney-Purta, 2004). Yet political knowledge is impacted by exposure to political information (Lynda, McKinney, & Tedesco, 2007), and internal political efficacy in youth and young adults has been found to be dependent on an individual's context, varying across the age spectrum (Beaumont, 2011; McFarland & Thomas, 2006; Torney-Purta et al., 2008). For example, in a study involving 116 interviews and over 600 surveys with youth and young adults, Kahne and Westheimer (2006) found that youth public service projects did not always improve the political efficacy of participants, and the frustrations with roadblocks experienced in service efforts could lead youth to experience frustration, hopelessness, and diminished intentions to politically engage (e.g., voting). In contrast, a later study by Kahne and Sporte (2008) of over 4,000 high school students in Chicago found that students who engaged civic learning opportunities that involved activities like discussions of current events or service learning experienced increases in their commitment to civic participation including solving problems in their community. Thus internal political efficacy is not exclusively or even necessarily an outcome of age or human development, but rather the result of experiences that support or dampen outcomes. The contexts and experiences work to construct new ways of knowing, building individual and collective capacities to understand and act (Baker, Jensen, & Kolb, 2005; Kolb, 1984; Kolb & Kolb, 2008).

Although large variation in the internal political efficacy measure did not exist across youth in the four programs examined, the interviews unearthed variation in the depth and complexity of how each teen understood social change, political engagement processes, and their role in leading such endeavors. In addition to internal political efficacy, some teens demonstrated markers of external political efficacy (Bandura, 1997; Morrell, 2003; Wilkenfeld, Lauckhardt, & Torney-Purta, 2010) or the belief that their opinions or concerns could be expressed, heard, and responded to by those who cared about what they thought or by those in power.

A few teens had already moved from attitude to action and were addressing community issues by contributing to and participating in activities they cared about (e.g., educating community about school to prison pipeline). Some demonstrated a complex understanding of root causes of problems that were linked to larger systems (e.g., institutional racism). These teens also indicated that change was complex, hard, and took time. There were teens who understood change or action was a collective endeavor achieved by working together and building connections.

The teen interviews suggest that sociopolitical development is multifaceted and influenced by the experiences within these varied programs. Looking through the lens of youth development theories, the programs exhibited markers of multiple youth development models with no site representing a pure model. Yet, by integrating youth development models (see Table 5.2) three distinct developmental domains emerge: individual, group, and community. Echoing Bronfenbrenner's (1979) ecological systems theory, this combined map suggests that complex program designs and dynamics work at different levels to meet sociopolitical development outcomes.

Integration of the models illuminates movement from personal development toward involvement with others and the larger community or society, suggesting that political agency entails competence in all three domains. As McIntosh and Youniss (2010) wrote,

> ... the nature of political engagement calls for a socialization process that involves developing reasons to become involved, joining with like-minded others to work towards collective goals, and learning to interact with competing interest groups to mutually achievable solutions to political problems. (pp. 29–30)

This integration of youth development models is further informed by youth civic engagement theories that link political socialization to development along the life course (Sherrod, Torney-Purta, & Flanagan, 2010). It also reflects Westheimer and Kahne (2004) earlier conceptualizations of a good citizen—the personally responsible citizen (individual), the participatory citizen (group), the justice-oriented citizen (community). It is compatible with the processes articulated in the social justice youth development model as stages of awareness: self awareness, social awareness, and global awareness (Ginwright & James, 2002). The integration also highlights how growing political agency and leadership support the dual purposes of individual development as well as building capacity within group and social domains that can lead to stronger social capital and collective outcomes (Bresso, 2012).

Snapshots of Political Learning Contexts

Each program explored works to build a specific set of skills and capacities in different developmental domains for the young people they serve. In some instances, the out-of-school-time program combined elements from more than one developmental domain. What follows is a brief description of how the four case examples build skills for political action and leadership for Boston teens.

The Empowering Family. Castle Square's Teen Center works to bolster youth and build them up as assets. It works primarily in the domain of the individual, helping to bridge the group domain. The empowering family focuses on creating a normative culture of care, comfort, welcome, and

Table 5.2 Youth Development (YD) Models by Developmental Domain

Domain	Social YD	Positive YD	Community YD	Social justice YD
Individual	Opportunities for productive prosocial roles Clear standards or norms for behavior Prevention of conduct problems—truancy, drug abuse, teen pregnancy Skills and competencies to be successfully involved in these roles—intelligence, resilience	Opportunities to learn healthy behaviors Emphasizing youths' strengths/challenging to build competence	Creating safe space Finding and living one's true calling. Transferring practical, usable skills	Identity central
Group	Bonding to prosocial family, school and peers Consistent systems of recognition and reinforcement	Promoting positive peer relationships Connecting youth with caring adults	Being conscious relationship stewards Creating a culture of appreciation Creating a culture of respect and partnership	Embraces youth culture
Community		Empowering youth to lead programs	Creating a just and compassionate society	Analyzes power in social relationships Promotes systemic social change Encourages collective action

Adapted from Ginwright and Cammarota (2002); Ginwright and James (2002); Hughes and Curnan (2002); Lerner (2005).

openness. Relationships between youth as well as between youth and adults are important in creating social bonds and trust. Adults may position themselves as mentors, guides, older siblings, or the quintessential good parent. There is a focus on individual development informed by theories of social and positive youth development. However, it pays particular attention to supporting youth voice, individual choice, and agency maintained through a highly responsive and adaptive stance toward the needs of participants. Youth are challenged and provided multiple levels at which to contribute to the organization and the larger community, which finds inspiration from the community youth development model.

The Team-Oriented Workplace. Friends of Beardsley Park's Youth Park Stewards works at building youth assets within the context of a group environment with steps toward connecting to a set of larger community concerns. It pulls from the social, positive, and community youth development models. The structure of the program is less fluid than that of the Empowering Family and motivation may initially be externally driven (e.g., paycheck). This type of program has expectations for how youth will conduct themselves and aspires for individuals to be productive team members. Adults in this model, while supportive and approachable, are more like good bosses than good parents. The team-oriented workplace consciously builds interpersonal skills while at the same time connecting work to larger social purposes, the primary focus of community youth development model. Contributions to community benefit are made visible.

The Liberation School. Youth Lead at the State Street Institute has a focus on pushing the individual to see the forces shaping our world. The liberation school pays attention to acquisition of new knowledge as well as practical skill development in leadership. This emphasis comes from its grounding in social justice youth development. Although this type of program continues to support the individual and group domains, it primarily works at building the skills necessary for individuals to be civic actors and social change agents. In these cases it finds affinity with positive and community youth development. The liberation school allows program participants to learn and grow as people toward leadership. This type of program trusts young people with power and continues to build bonds through confronting difference and oppression. Skills in critical awareness and thinking are also built. Adults position themselves as facilitators, guides, and resources. Again, all of these are clearly informed by the social justice youth development model.

The Citizenship Guild. Centro Cultural Latino's Community Organizers works to integrate development of all three domains (individual, group, and community) through a commitment to long-term engagement with the individual. It works to create a caring environment where young people feel welcomed as a hallmark of social and positive youth development strategies. The citizenship guild wants program participants to be aware of their own personal development and growth, which comes from theories of positive youth development. It wants youth to achieve and be productive. Youth develop connections to others both within the organization and the community (i.e., social capital) linking it to community youth development. It works to consciously build skills and competence in all domains and provides support across the organization. It links youth to other actors in the community as well as those in power, which draws some lessons from social justice youth development.

These organizing metaphors are not the only ones possible. They simply detail how different youth development models express themselves to varying degrees within program contexts and work to build the capacities of different development domains: individual, group, and community. Programs might primarily focus on one developmental domain, but may have program elements that work in other developmental domains. A program might work to combine skills development in all three developmental domains. It is also possible that youth might build skills and capacities in one environment and build on others in a different location (e.g., families, schools, work).

A Multifaceted Political Leadership Learning Ecosystem

Teens from the two organizations with programs articulating strong, well-articulated youth development and leadership models, Centro Cultural Latino and State Street Institute, demonstrate knowledge about larger social issues addressed by these programs, such as cultural competency, public health, and racial discrimination. Their concrete experiences in civic and political action within their community (e.g., door-to-door canvassing, community education, speaking to those in power about community issues) are more pronounced than teens in the other two programs. Yet, teens at both the Friends of Beardsley Park and the Castle Square have insights into larger social issues and systems. Stephanie at Castle Square's Teen Center speaks in depth about ethnic and gender stereotypes:

> ... you have to have your own thoughts, you cannot follow everybody else's chain of thoughts. Have your own chain of thinking, have your own perspective of things, have self-respect for you. ... You don't always have to be a stereotype. For me, I felt like I'm always trying to avoid my stereotype. ... For me it's like I hate stereotypes about my race. (personal communication, August 31, 2011)

JD at the Friends was earlier quoted in this chapter expressing a critical perspective on cultural assumptions regarding natural resources and consumption of material goods. Teens at both Castle Square and Friends note connections to the larger community through participation in community events and projects, even if these experiences are not framed within a context of political action. The teens in these two programs demonstrate other elements of learning related to political agency skills and attitudes. For example, youth hanging out at Castle Square's Teen Center express incredibly strong youth voice, individual agency, and social bonding. This is despite the lack of a formal training program or a conscious youth development model seeking such outcomes for teens. BD explains how learning dance moves from his Teen Center peer Ben and then performing in the community built up his confidence:

> I don't know I always found it embarrassing out in public just doing whatever. I mean I was always very self-conscious about my movements and what I could do. And then I saw Ben do it, and it's like, "Yeah, I'll try it" ... less self-conscious about being in front of a whole lot of people, yeah ... I would I have definitely said, "no" right off the bat ... You're in front of people. I never liked doing any of that. But I think, through dance, I was able to shake off the nervousness in front of people. I can even speak in front of a bunch of people now. (personal communication, September 30, 2011)

Taylor at Friends talks about how she and other teens collectively built raised community garden beds:

> We helped build six flowerbeds. We actually drilled the cardboard boxes together, like you know, the wood ... to make the flowerbeds and then we laid down the plastic underneath it and soil, so that the people in the apartment building, they'd have fresh vegetables and stuff. (personal communication, August 10, 2011)

These capacities and experiences associated with self-efficacy, or "the confidence in one's ability to control and execute the actions required to deal with current and future situations" (Wilkenfeld et al., 2010, p.195), and collective efficacy, "a group's shared belief in its conjoint capabilities to organize and execute the course of action required to produce given levels of attainment" (Bandura, 1997, p. 477), are linked to civic and political participation in future life (Hart, Donnelly, Younuiss, & Atkins, 2007; Wilkenfeld et al., 2010; Youniss & Yates, 1997). So clearly, these two organizations are involved in developing political agency and leadership outcomes not consciously articulated in program objectives.

At the other end of the spectrum, the State Street Institute's program of critical consciousness raising and efforts to train young people to see the systemic roots of social problems is not as successful with the most struggling teens. As explained by Institute co-director Bert Myles,

> ... assessments reveal that participants in the Youth Lead program seem to need a base level of social justice interest or leadership capacity for the program to have a positive impact on their development. So not just any teen is

best recruited into the Youth Lead program. One size does not fit all students. (personal communication, July 20, 2011)

The theoretical literature suggests that individuals start the process of political agency and engagement at different places and thus need different strategies and learning environments based on their interests, skills, and capacities (McIntosh & Youniss, 2010; Wilkenfeld et al., 2010). Schools interested in civic and political engagement are encouraged to offer a range of cocurricular activities to meet the diverse civic and political learning needs of students (Finley, Wray-Lake, & Flanagan, 2010; Jonathan, Levine, McConnell, & Smith, 2011). It follows that community organizations need to provide diverse opportunities out of school for young people to become politically socialized as actors and leaders (CIRCLE, 2013; Finley et al., 2010; Westheimer & Kahne, 2004). Youth need diverse opportunities to provide multiple entry points and pathways, allowing them flexibility to move along the sociopolitical development continuum. Youth benefit from engaging in different activities and interventions, even at different organizations or in different types of programs within the same organization (McIntosh & Youniss, 2010).

Insights from this exploration suggest that youth do not need an ideal programmatic design informed by a singular youth development model serving monolithic sociopolitical and leadership development needs. The ability to envision a better society and have the knowledge, skill, and confidence to decide and act can be learned in diverse contexts. To put young people on a pathway toward political agency and civic leadership begins with bolstering the individual and building on this foundation to include skills within group contexts, and then transitioning youth into the wider spheres of community and the larger society over the course of one's life (Sherrod et al., 2010). At each stage, youth continue to build and strengthen their capacities in existing domains. Out-of-school-time programs can work to move young people along this pathway.

With an integrated set of youth development models disaggregated along developmental domains—individual, group, and community—programs select a range of strategies to meet the specific needs of the youth population they serve. Rather than employ one youth development model, programs mix and match from multiple models. In this way, the path to civic leadership begins with the building of an individual's skills and capacities related to political knowledge, confidence, voice, and agency. As these skills are built, one moves into ever-increasing wider scope of engagement (see Figure 5.1). Individuals move from small intimate groups such as family and friends to more public groups such as work and school. In doing so, they add to their individual repertoires new skills and abilities that allow them to engage with others. Listening, collaborating, coordinating, cooperating, deliberating, entering into and resolving conflict, compromising, and acting collectively are practiced and developed. As these small group

Figure 5.1.   Sociopolitical Development Pathway

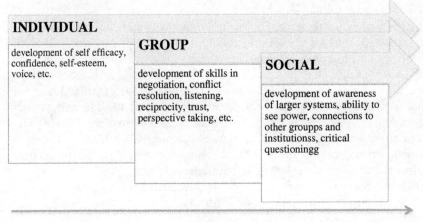

INDIVIDUAL

development of self efficacy, confidence, self-esteem, voice, etc.

GROUP

development of skills in negotiation, conflict resolution, listening, reciprocity, trust, perspective taking, etc.

SOCIAL

development of awareness of larger systems, ability to see power, connections to other groupps and institutionss, critical questioningg

TIME

skills are built, attention to an individual's holistic development continues. Moving into the larger spheres of community and society, youth develop the ability to work for the benefit of the community; to see and empathize with positions that are not their own; to understand large systems; and to assess and evaluate social, cultural, political, and economic systems, as well as power, critically. This is a multilayered development process.

The programs in the study are consistent with leadership development as a multi-sphere endeavor (Brass, 2001; Bresso, 2012; Hitt & Ireland, 2002; Kline, 2003). With an orientation toward political engagement, the programs demonstrate that building individual skills and capacities work toward and in concert with more collective and community capacities (Azzam & Riggio, 2003; Cress et al., 2001). With a base of internal political efficacy, the teens in the study strengthen their individual voice and self-efficacy, gain the ability to work with others to achieve individual and collective goals, and improve their understanding of public issues and the means to act positively upon them. They have taken the first step toward becoming political agents and civic leaders.

References

Azzam, T., & Riggio, R. E. (2003). Community based civic leadership: A descriptive investigation. *Journal of Leadership and Organizational Studies, 10*(1), 55–67.

Baker, A. C., Jensen, P. J., & Kolb, D. A. (2005). Conversation as experiential learning. *Management Learning, 36*, 411–427.

Bandura, A. (1997). *Self-efficacy: The exercise of control.* New York, NY: Macmillan.

Beaumont, E. (2011). Promoting political agency, addressing political inequality: A multilevel model of internal political efficacy. *The Journal of Politics, 73*(1), 216–231.

Brass, D. J. (2001). Social capital and organizational leadership. In S. J. Zaccaro & R. J. Klimoski (Eds.), *The nature of organizational leadership: Understanding the performance imperatives confronting today's leaders* (pp. 132–152). San Francisco, CA: Jossey Bass.

Bresso, M. (2012). *Building for the future: Community college leadership development program evaluation.* Retrieved from ProQuest Dissertations & Theses Global (Order No. 3549739).

Bronfenbrenner, U. (1979). *The ecology of human development: Experiments by nature and design.* Cambridge, MA: Harvard University Press.

CIRCLE. (2013). *All together now: Collaboration and innovation for youth engagement.* Commission on Youth Voting and Civic Knowledge. Medford, MA: Center for Information & Research on Civic Learning and Engagement. Retrieved from www.civicyouth.org/about-circle/commission-on-youth-voting-civic-knowledge/

Clyde, C. (2010). Developing civic leaders through an experiential learning programme for Holocaust education. *Prospects, 40,* 289–306.

Cress, C. M., Astin, H. S., Zimmerman-Oster, K., & Burkhardt, J. C. (2001). Developmental outcomes of college students' involvement in leadership activities. *Journal of College Student Development, 42,* 15–27.

Finley, A., Wray-Lake, L., & Flanagan, C. (2010). Civic engagement during the transition to adulthood: Developmental opportunities and social politics at a critical juncture. In L. R. Sherrod, J. Torney-Purta, & C. Flanagan (Eds.), *Handbook on research of civic engagement in youth* (pp. 277–305). Hoboken, NJ: Wiley.

Ginwright, S., & Cammarota, J. (2002). New terrain in youth development:The promise of a social justice approach. *Social Justice, 29*(4), 82–95.

Ginwright, S., & James, T. (2002, Winter). From assets to agents of change: Social justice, organizing, and youth development. *New Directions for Youth Development, 96,* 27–46.

Giroux, H. (2005). Translating the future, review of education. *Pedagogy & Cultural Studies, 27*(3), 213–218.

Hart, D., Donnelly, T. M., Youniss, J., & Atkins, R. (2007). High school community service as a predictor of adult voting and volunteering. *American Educational Research Journal, 44*(1),197–219.

Hitt, M. A., & Ireland, R. D. (2002). The essence of strategic leadership: Managing human and social capital. *Journal of Leadership and Organizational Studies, 9*(1), 3–14.

Hughes, D. M., & Curnan, S. P. (2002). Community youth development: A framework for action. *Community Youth Development Journal, 1*(1). Retrieved from http://www.youthpolicy.org/research/journals/community-youth-development-journal/

Jonathan, K. H., Levine, P., McConnell, T., & Smith, D. B. (Eds.). (2011). *Guardian of democracy: The civic mission of schools.* Philadelphia, PA: Leonore Annenberg Institute for Civics of the Annenberg Public Policy Center at the University of Pennsylvania.

Kahne, J., & Sporte, S. E. (2008). Developing citizens: The impact of civic learning opportunities on students' commitment to civic participation. *American Educational Research Journal, 45,* 738–766.

Kahne, J., & Westheimer, J. (2006). The limits of political efficacy: Educating citizens for a democratic society. *PS: Political Science & Politics, 39,* 289–296.

Keating, E., Pradhan, G., Wasall, G. H., & DeNatale, D. (2008). *Passion and purpose: Raising the fiscal fitness bar for Massachusetts nonprofits.* Boston, MA: The Boston Foundation. Retrieved from http://www.tbf.org/~/media/TBFOrg/Files/Reports/PassionPurpose%20Raising%20the%20Fiscal%20Fitness.pdf

Kline, T. (2003). *Teams that lead: A matter of market strategy, leadership skills, and executive strength.* New York, NY: Wiley.

Kolb, A. Y., & Kolb, D. A. (2008). Experiential learning theory: A dynamic, holistic approach to management learning, education, and development. In S. J. Armstrong

& C. Fukami (Eds.), *Handbook of management learning, education and development* (pp. 42–68). London: Sage Publications.

Kolb, D. A. (1984). *Experiential learning: Experience as the source of learning and development*. Englewood Cliffs, NJ: Prentice-Hall.

Kress, C. A. (2006). Youth leadership and youth development: Connections and questions. In M. Klau, S. Boyd, L. Luckow, & Associates. *Youth leadership. New Directions for Youth Development* (No. 109, pp. 45–56). San Francisco, CA: Jossey-Bass.

Lerner, R. (2005). Promoting positive youth development: Theoretical and empirical bases, paper prepared for Workshop on the Science of Adolescent Health and Development, National Research Council / Institute of Medicine, Washington, DC. September 9, 2005. Washington, DC: National Academy of Sciences. Retrieved from http://ase.tufts.edu/iaryd/documents/pubPromotingPositive.pdf

Lynda, L. K., McKinney, M. S., & Tedesco, J. C. (2007). Introduction: Political information efficacy and young voters. *The American Behavioral Scientist, 50*(9), 1093–1111.

Massachusetts Nonprofit Database. (2010). *Nonprofit organizations by industry sector.* Retrieved from http://nccsdataweb.urban.org/PubApps/nonprofit-overview-sumRpt .php?v=ntee&t=pc&f=0

McFarland, D. A., & Thomas, R. J. (2006). Bowling young: How youth voluntary associations influence adult political participation. *American Sociological Review, 71*(3), 401–425.

McIntosh, H., & Youniss, J. (2010). Toward a political theory of political socialization of youth. In L. R. Sherrod, J. Torney-Purta, & C. Flanagan (Eds.), *Handbook on research of civic engagement in youth* (pp. 23–24). Hoboken, NJ: Wiley.

Morrell, M. M. (2003). Survey and experimental evidence for a reliable and valid measure of internal political efficacy. *Public Opinion Quarterly, 67,* 589–602.

Roberts, D. C. (2007). *Deeper learning in leadership: Helping college students find the potential within.* San Francisco, CA: Jossey Bass.

Sherrod, L., Torney-Purta, J., & Flanagan, C. (2010). Introduction to research on the development of citizenship: A field comes of age. In L. R. Sherrod, J. Torney-Purta, & C. Flanagan (Eds.), *Handbook on research of civic engagement in youth* (pp. 1–22). Hoboken, NJ: Wiley.

Torney-Purta, J. (2004, June). Adolescents' political socialization in changing contexts: An international study in the spirit of Nevitt Sanford [Special issue, part two]. *Political Psychology, 25*(3), 465–478.

Torney-Purta, J., Wilkenfeld, B., & Barber, C. (2008). How adolescents in 27 countries understand, support, and practice human rights. *Journal of Social Issues, 64,* 857–880.

Westheimer, J., & Kahne, J. (2004). What kind of citizen: The politics of educating for democracy. *American Educational Research Journal, 41*(2), 237–269.

Wheeler, W., & Edlebeck, C. (2006). Leading, learning, and unleashing potential: Youth leadership and civic engagement. In M. Klau, S. Boyd, L. Luckow, & Associates. *Youth leadership. New Directions for Youth Development* (No. 109, pp. 89–97). San Francisco, CA: Jossey-Bass.

Wilkenfeld, B., Lauckhardt, J., & Torney-Purta, J. (2010). The relation between developmental theory and measures of civic engagement in research on adolescents. In L. R. Sherrod, J. Torney-Purta, & C. Flanagan (Eds.), *Handbook on research of civic engagement in youth* (pp. 193–219). Hoboken, NJ: Wiley.

Youniss, J., & Yates, M. (1997). *Community service and social responsibility in youth.* Chicago, IL: The University of Chicago Press.

FELICIA M. SULLIVAN *is senior researcher at the Center for Information and Research on Civic Learning and Engagement (CIRCLE) housed at the Jonathan M. Tisch College of Citizenship and Public Service at Tufts University.*

*This chapter examines two global education programs in higher
education, one in the global North and the other in the global South
to explore the shift from command to community in leadership.*

Educating for Global Leadership:
A North–South Collaboration

Nicholas V. Longo, Janice McMillan

A recent report by the World Economic Forum about the global outlook for
2015 found "lack of leadership" among the most pressing global issues—
after only "economic inequality" and "persistent jobless growth"—with a
striking 86% of survey respondents from around the world agreeing that
we have a leadership crisis (Petriglieri, 2014). At the same time, there is
also a shift occurring in our beliefs regarding where that leadership needs
to come from. There is growing recognition of the limitations of the traditional notion of the top-down charismatic leader. Complex global issues
like climate change, economic inequality, or urban poverty are not going
to be resolved with technical fixes or individuals working in isolation; they
require new ways of thinking and acting—and leading.

A new generation of young people with changing definitions of leadership in a changing world is also emerging. They are not interested in charismatic leaders showing them the way; they want to do it themselves or in
partnership with others (Longo & Gibson, 2011). Added to this, these im-
pulses are coming not only from the global North, but also more forcefully
from the global South—and with increasing urgency. Movements on university campuses in South Africa, for instance, are growing all the time. One
recent example is Inkulufreeheid, a national student movement started on a
university campus in 2013, aiming to "unite all South Africans, particularly
young people, behind non-partisan efforts that help solve major economic
challenges, deepen democracy and enhance social cohesion" (Gauteng &
Eastern Cape, 2013).

Research shows that young people increasingly see ordinary people
as being better equipped to solve their problems than authority figures
or experts. They are also more likely to have ambivalent, even negative

NEW DIRECTIONS FOR STUDENT LEADERSHIP, no. 148, Winter 2015 © 2015 Wiley Periodicals, Inc., A Wiley Company
Published online in Wiley Online Library (wileyonlinelibrary.com) • DOI: 10.1002/yd.20154

feelings about formal leadership, preferring horizontal arrangements where everyone takes responsibility for leadership (Hart Research Associates, 1998; Longo & Gibson, 2011). As one student involved with a civic leadership program explained, "I've learned that, yes I could lead a group of people, one me and all the rest followers, I could do that." The student continued with the conception of leadership that permeates the model of leadership we will explore in this essay: "But how much better would it be if it was a room full of leaders?" (Longo & Gibson, 2011).

This chapter builds upon this understanding of leadership by examining two global education programs in higher education, one in the global North, the other in the global South. These programs are focused on developing student leadership through civic engagement in colleges and universities. The programs we direct at Providence College and the University of Cape Town, South Africa (UCT), in very different contexts, reinforce the importance of a new definition of leadership education that values transparency, authenticity, collaboration, action, and interactivity. This new leadership is part of a shift from command and control, to community and reciprocity, framed by a concern for social justice—a change that can be found in the approaches to citizen leadership education across the globe.

Citizen Leadership

The failure of the traditional model of leadership is becoming more evident—while the need for something different becomes more pressing. Carne Ross, a former British diplomat who resigned over the invasion of Iraq, takes this up this theme in his prescient reflections on what he terms "the leaderless revolution." Realizing that current government structures are not up to the task, Ross (2011) writes:

> What is needed is a much more fundamental, wholly new method of doing things. No longer should we look for change to emerge from untrusted politicians, arguing in distant chambers ... We have to accept the painful reality that we can no longer rely on government policy to solve our most deep-seated and intractable problems, from climate change to social alienation. Instead, we need to look to ourselves for the necessary action. (p. xvii)

Assessments like this reinforce the need for a different kind of leadership. Political theorist Benjamin Barber (1998) takes up this challenge by attempting to change dominant conceptions of leadership in democracy, arguing that in a strong democracy there is a need for strong citizens, not strong leaders. Barber's point is that when leadership is defined by finding charismatic individuals, the result is disempowered citizens. In South Africa's new democracy, this has been echoed in many quarters. Cyril Ramaphosa, South African Deputy President and Founding Patron of the global leadership network Common Purpose, argues that South Africans cannot wait for great ideas from great people to solve their problems, but must look to one another to transform their country (Middleton, 2007).

Thus, the success of democracy comes not in finding great individual leaders, but in acknowledging the leadership and knowledge in all citizens. This concept of leadership has strong roots in the South African anti-Apartheid and U.S. civil rights struggles, practices especially worth noting because of the presence of legendary charismatic leaders at the forefront of these movements in Nelson Mandela and Martin Luther King, Jr., respectively. "In most public treatments, movement leaders take on gigantic, even superhuman proportions, while the people become radically diminished," explains Harry Boyte (2014b), a leading scholar on citizen-centered politics (p. 3). But the stories of leadership in these struggles are much more rich and complicated, offering precursors to the model of leadership we are describing. Boyte (2014b) continues,

> The dominant story holds that Martin Luther King gave a speech and Congress abolished segregation. Nelson Mandela got out of jail and negotiated the end to apartheid ... What is lost is the immense creativity, energy, and spirit of everyday citizens, as well as the molecular transformations in communities and institutions that made these movements successful. (p. 3–4)

This theme is also articulated by King's colleague (and sometimes critic) Ella Baker, an organizer for the Southern Christian Leadership Conference (SCLC). Baker argued against leadership as coming from a "magic man," and instead as "individuals who are bound together by a concept that benefited the larger number of individuals and provided an opportunity for them to grow" (quoted in Ransby, 2003, p. 188). As she rather provocatively put it, "strong people don't need strong leaders" (Ransby, 2003, p. 188).

Likewise, in reflecting on what can be learned from South African social movements, Boyte (2014a) writes: "The real lesson is that it takes a great array of talents and capacities, not a superhero or a saint, to make large scale democratic change" (para. 2). This lesson is supported by the research of Xolela Mangcu, a public scholar at the UCT, who argues that if South Africa wishes to create a "a more participatory democracy built on strong community foundations" it requires "a departure from the over-reliance on 'big leaders' and their technocratic solutions that has characterized South African society both pre and post-apartheid" (Mangcu, 2012, p. 297).

South African scholars continue to make the case for the development of students as citizen leaders. In a recent publication on higher-education transformation in South Africa, Leibowitz et al. (2012) argue that attributes such as "compassion, criticality and a sense of responsibility" are necessary to enable students to contribute toward "civic reconciliation and transformation" (p. xi). Soudien (2006) brings past and present together in writing about the relationship between education and citizenship, stating that there are two positions: the need to teach young people their history and culture in order to "build their dignity and feelings of self-worth" (p. 114), and the need for education to provide young people with the "high skills knowledge" (p. 114)—the cultural capital—that will enable them to operate within the complexity of a globalized world. Soudien argues we must give students a sense of local history as well as a connection to kinds of knowledge that can enable them to become citizen leaders.

Higher Education and the Global Ecology of Education

A growing number of observers have called on universities to play a more active role in educating the leaders we need in the 21st century. A report for the Kellogg Foundation argues that, "colleges and universities provide rich opportunities for recruiting and developing leaders through the curriculum and co-curriculum" (Astin & Astin, 2000, p. 3). Leadership Reconsidered declares:

> If the next generation of citizen leaders is to be engaged and committed to leading for the common good, then the institutions which nurture them must be engaged in the work of the society and the community, modeling effective leadership and problem solving skills, demonstrating how to accomplish change for the common good. (Astin & Astin, 2000, p. 2)

As the world becomes more connected, leaders will also have to be more adept at transcending the self and reaching out and working with others in a larger community/external setting. Colleges and universities, many of which already require service-learning or community-based research from students, can build on these efforts by linking them with a deeper model of leadership education that emphasizes civic engagement as fundamental to leadership (Longo & Gibson, 2011).

However, also needed in an interconnected world are more global North–South collaborations for students across the globe to learn from and with each other. Through our own collaboration, we have begun to understand our interdependencies. Although too often global challenges are targeted toward saving the global South, the world more broadly is facing a series of complex issues, and new leadership is needed that focuses on global collaborations among a diverse mix of stakeholders.

Developing such an understanding of leadership involves recognizing what educational historian Lawrence Cremin (1976) termed the "ecology of education," which finds that education takes place outside the boundaries of a classroom in multiple settings in a web of learning. In educating for global leadership, learners and educators can think globally, regardless of whether the community-based learning is taking place in local or international settings by acknowledging the interconnectedness of these communities. But when students can engage in global leadership programs outside of their home cultures, even greater outcomes may be possible. Adam Weinberg and his colleagues (Hovey, Weinberg, & Bellamy, 2011) utilize the School of International Training (SIT) Study Abroad Programs to propose a "global ecology of learning" in which students learn through deep cultural immersion in communities. They note that this way of thinking "can be used as a guiding concept" for "educational activities beyond the borders of our local communities and nation" (Hovey et al., 2011, p. 39). They conclude that "much of the gain as global citizens may actually take place through the reentry process" (Hovey et al., 2011, p. 43), continuing that this is where "students come back with the commitments and capacities to engage in public work across national and cultural differences in order to create a better world" (Hovey et al., 2011, p. 46).

Students as Global Citizen–Leaders: A North–South Perspective. Our programs at Providence College and UCT prepare students to be global citizens and leaders. While organized differently to address the unique cultures of our campuses, each is part of a growing effort in leadership learning that emphasizes "relationship over position" and "action over attainment" (Mitchell, Visconti, Keene, & Battistoni, 2011, p. 115). At Providence College, student leadership is built into an interdisciplinary Global Studies major, where students often cofacilitate courses with faculty members and work side-by-side with community partners in global issues locally and internationally. At UCT, students develop leadership skills that enable them to grapple with issues of development, poverty, and inequality through involvement in broad-ranging debates and community projects in UCT Global Citizenship: Leading for Social Justice Program (GCP; Hovey et al., 2011).

These programs—described below—are part of a wave of leadership programs prioritizing action and public purpose, as opposed to position and authority. As a result, leadership is understood as something that is measured not by individual accomplishments or personal success, but rather by how civil society and communities are served. A student in the UCT Global Citizenship program commented:

> It is important not to let our professions make us inconsiderate of the communities that we serve. For instance, in my field of study, Civil Engineering, my job will be about helping improve people's lives. It will be important for me to make sure that the different communities that I am going to serve have a voice and that their voice is heard. (McMillan, 2013, p. 36)

This leadership ethos emphasizes collaboration and horizontal arrangements in which everyone is a leader, more bottom-up than top-down, and inclusive in welcoming diversity in all its facets. In short, there is a shift to a new model of global leadership education.

Global Studies at Providence College. Global Studies is an interdisciplinary major preparing the next generation to engage responsibly with our increasingly interconnected world. This is accomplished through a curriculum that requires learners to develop sensitivity to local cultures and identities as they build their capacity to act as global problem solvers and engaged citizen leaders (García & Longo, 2013). The curriculum focuses on providing a sustained, developmental, integrated experience in which students

- take foundational courses, including research methods, which include local community engagement
- study interdisciplinary areas such as international politics, the philosophy of globalization, cross-cultural communication, world religions, and the global economy
- have an immersion experience outside the United States, which includes an internship, action research project, or service-learning course
- design a thematic concentration in a self-selected area of global studies, and
- conclude with advanced courses in global studies and foreign language, including a year-long capstone course that includes a collaborative action project, often in the local community

From the beginning, Global Studies has focused on understanding the intersection of the local and international through experiential learning and leadership in the Providence community and around the world. As one student explains,

> Global Studies is constantly using the city of Providence as a classroom. I have had so many opportunities to see the community that surrounds our college as a microcosm of the world, and to make connections between the global issues that I find most interesting—like immigration, for example—and real people they affect. (García & Longo, 2013, p. 39–40)

Integrating local service in an international service-learning course enhances students' understanding and appreciation of the interconnected world—essential for the study of globalization. Moreover, local–global engagement provides significant opportunities to participate responsibly in community problem solving and reflective practice.

Students also play significant leadership roles, including serving on advisory and hiring committees, coteaching courses, and acting as liaisons between service learners and community partners. Further, the Global Studies major emphasizes the citizen-centered model of leadership described above. As such, courses are taught in a participatory style, where all voices, experiences, and knowledge are valued. Upper-level students are often included on the facilitation team in courses, enabling a cascading model of leadership. Students also act as formal community liaisons with community partners, a position that offers a small stipend and ongoing training for students who act as volunteer coordinators and reflection leaders at globally focused community sites, such as a local international language immersion charter school, an adult education program for new immigrants that utilizes democratic educational practices, and an organization that supports the resettlement of recent refugees.

Global Citizenship Program at the University of Cape Town.   The UCT Global Citizenship: Leading for Social Justice Program (GCP) was launched in 2010 to help meet the University's strategic goals, including enhancing the quality and profile of graduates, becoming an "Afropolitan" university, and expanding and enhancing UCT's contribution to South Africa's development challenges. The broad program objectives are:

- To expose students to global citizenship and social justice issues beyond degree or discipline
- To develop capacity for leadership on contemporary global–political and social justice issues by improving active listening, critical thinking, and logical argument
- To promote awareness of themselves as future global citizens motivated to work for social justice through community service/volunteering

The GCP is open to all students from all faculties and levels of study. At the core of the program are three cocurricular short courses: Global Debates, Local Voices (GC1), Service, Citizenship, and Social Justice (GC2), and 60 hours of self-organized community service with structured reflection (GC3). There is also a credit-bearing course in engineering open to all students reflecting components of GC1 and GC2. Because of the need to be flexible and fit in with students' academic responsibilities, the courses have developed strong on-line learning components. In the past 5 years, over 1,000 students from across all faculties and disciplines as well as from a range of different countries in Africa have participated in at least one of the GCP short courses.

The GCP provides students with skills—underpinned explicitly by the values of social justice—that will broaden their perspectives and develop their leadership capacities while encouraging them to make links between self and the local and global contexts in which they find themselves. In particular, an awareness of social justice issues is a first step toward identifying the realms of the possible and aspirational within particular personal, institutional, and broader contexts. The program frames leadership education as occurring across three domains of learning, action, and reflection: self, organizations or mediating agencies, and broader context and community. GCP fosters an understanding of their intersection and how each domain relates to core issues of social justice and engaged citizenship. The program encourages students to locate themselves in each of these three domains as a way to identify both the opportunities and constraints that inform what they can do as individuals who are organizationally and institutionally located within a broader structural context. As students engage and develop leadership skills, knowledge, and values across the intersection of these three domains, the goal is that social justice becomes the linking concept.

The GCP engages students as scholars, leaders, and citizens who are keen to learn, think about, critique, and respond to key contemporary issues. Given its African context, the program brings social justice into the framing of questions, and uses this lens throughout to think about how we might be responsive to and for the world in which we live (Beall, McMillan, & Small, 2010). GCP is thus concerned both with the global and its connections with the local, and two of the short courses look at these issues albeit in slightly different way. The first (Global Debates, Local Voices) considers global issues first and asks how these are realized or represented locally; the second (Service, Citizenship, and Social Justice) focuses more specifically on how, in our engagement and partnerships with local communities, there exists the potential to mirror global dynamics and power relationships in microcosm. At both levels the program challenges students to confront the centrality of power and social injustice in local and global relationships utilizing the work of global leaders, such as Paul Farmer (2005), to make these issues come alive.

As a result, GCP develops students as leaders who take seriously the issues of power and inequality and who are not afraid to challenge the dominant paradigms. A civil engineering student illustrates the kind of leadership being developed through GCP:

> As a Civil Engineering student I have found that we occupy a very interesting space in that we have to be technically minded while appreciating that our endeavors, once we are in the work environment, shall have a direct impact on people's lives. GCP has allowed me to re-examine where I see myself within the world and critically evaluate the ideas I have about development, and those we so often unjustifiably see as the 'Other' when we think about such engagements. It has challenged this thinking and subtly appealed to my sense of humanity, leading me to resist a gung-ho approach to issues of social justice. (J. McMillan, personal communication, 2012)

It is this kind of leadership that the GCP is working to develop: a leadership that will equip students to deal with turbulence, inequality, and uncertainty in the global world at large, often manifested in a local context.

Emerging Promising Practices for Global Education

Martha Nussbaum (2007) asks: if our universities are graduating citizens, what kind of citizens are they graduating? What kinds of knowledge, skills, and values are our students—as future leaders locally and globally— acquiring in their university education? These questions seem timely, given our efforts at Providence College and UCT. By considering some of the emerging promising practices for global citizenship education in higher education—such as the need for a focus on social justice, for student leadership to accompany local and global communities in their own development process, and for opportunities for global North–South collaborations for students and faculty alike—we can begin to see practices that need to be central to develop global leaders in university education. This, of course, is not an exhaustive but a preliminary exploration, based on an analysis of our programs. We hope others can expand these ideas.

Practicing a Leadership Focused on Social Justice. "Like playing soccer, building furniture, or baking bread, leadership is a practice," writes Knight Abowitz and her colleagues (Knight Abowitz, Raill-Jayanandhan, & Woiteshek, 2011, p. 87) at Miami University. "As a practice, it has a commonly recognizable set of certain activities associated with it … aimed at improving our lives in some way" (Knight Abowitz et al., 2011, p. 87). The practices of citizen leadership or global citizenship have both universal meanings as well as local significance. South Africa and Africa more broadly require engaging with social justice issues, from a global and local standpoint. Education therefore must not just focus on, but also must to be framed in response to injustice, so as to inform values and actions. Thus there is a need to frame leadership so that we can help students enact it in particular contexts. From our work, we believe that learning and education for global leadership provides an important lens on the world, a way of learning about and engaging in the world in new ways reflecting new forms of being, through which we can develop new sensitivities.

Global Studies at Providence College has developed a global service-learning program with partnerships in Providence and Latin America that focus on issues of social justice. One course, for instance, studies global coffee culture with a trip to coffee farms in Nicaragua, along with community-based research projects for a local coffee shop in Providence. Another set of global service-learning trips, to Ecuador and Nicaragua, respectively, included arts-based projects in Providence that culminated in a transnational arts exhibition around the theme of peace and justice. One student involved with these projects recognized that reflection, storytelling, and community partnerships are "the true backbone of global change and social justice" (Alonso García & Longo, 2015, p. 11).

Likewise, GCP is increasingly working to develop opportunities on the University campus for students to engage in actions that reflect a concern for social justice. Program leaders want students to have a different lens on the world, realizing that inequality and social justice issues exist on the UCT campus, not just in underresourced communities (e.g., students come from very different backgrounds and are not all privileged; workers on the campus have many struggles around working conditions). Following Nussbaum, the global leadership program is helping students live an examined life and providing opportunities for students to walk in the shoes of people very different from themselves, that can go some way toward cultivating a sense of humanity in our students going forward (Nussbaum, 2007). Reflecting this understanding, one GCP student leader states:

> I think that we should ask the question about poverty differently, precisely because changing the questions challenges our perceptions of the problem. That is important because our perceptions are often part of the problem: we disable/pacify people we think are helpless victims of poverty, but by focusing on these people, we let wealthier people off the hook, because they do not feature as part of the problem's definition or solution. (GCP student forum post, GC1 short course, 2013)

Accompanying Communities Through Leadership Education. Within the complex ecology of education, community engagement inevitably becomes a key component of educating for the new leadership. But civic engagement movements in higher education and civic engagement movements in communities are too often disconnected (Mathews, 2009). Thus, leadership education must learn to see community partnerships through a lens of reciprocity, with an approach that might be termed *accompanying communities*. Simonelli, Earle, and Story (2004) argue that we need an "understanding [of] how the community or neighborhood fits into the larger power environment or political landscape" (p. 54). In particular, they argue for service being to "[p]rovide long-term accompaniment to communities in their process of autonomous ... development" (p. 44).

Students learn that "to be involved with 'helping' autonomous communities meant that we must accompany them based on their guidelines or acompanar obediciendo" (Simonelli et al., 2004, p. 46). This captures our approaches about student leadership development: the need to help students not assume they are serving but to learn service (Boyle-Baise et al., 2006) as part of leadership so that they may accompany diverse communities on their own process of development as part of learning about leadership (McMillan & Stanton, 2014).

Focusing on accompaniment—and learning service—means being able to reflect critically upon potentially disabling and disempowering aspects of campus–community partnerships. This is a central component of the GCP in South Africa, where students immerse themselves in issues of power and inequality. In UCT's short course, two of the classes take place in the community and with community participants as colearners. This provides a real context for the students' learning. Based on such experiences, a student leader reflected:

> Development is a team effort. This is must not be interpreted as undermining the value and importance of university qualifications but rather what I intend to put across is that the work done by the "experts" in communities would/can be much more effective if the communities are given a voice in the process of their development. (McMillan, 2013, p. 36)

Issues emerging from the accompaniment of communities are also central in the Global Studies major at Providence College, where the concept of *eloquent listening* is core to the campus–community partnerships that occur in all of the courses. One Global Studies student reflects, "Service makes the problems of the world real. Experiences bring this learning to a 'real' level. You need to listen" (García & Longo, 2013, p. 48). This is often done through community partnerships, both local and international. For instance, a recent course focused on listening to the stories of youth in Providence and in Nicaragua as part of a global service-learning course. With the use of mediums such as interviewing and photography, students worked with youth in Nicaragua and Providence to accompany community partners through stories. One student summed up this up by connecting stories, accompaniment, and empowerment:

> The voices that are too often silenced are voices that come from developing countries that have seen firsthand what discrimination and oppression looks like. I feel that if the world begins to listen more closely to these voices, powerful change can be made. (Alonso García & Longo, 2015, p. 1)

Engaging in North–South Collaborations

Finally, universities across North and South need to find ways for students and faculty to learn from and engage with each other. This links to the idea of the global ecology of education discussed earlier. However, such a process of learning and engagement with "the other" might require unlearning dominant paradigms and assumptions (Morphet, 1992). In many university contexts, this is not easy, as institutions, together with their students and faculty, are often resistant to change. It gets more complex and uncomfortable when the issues are linked to power, inequality, and social justice. The work of Nigerian author Chimamanda Adichie (2009) addresses this through what she terms as the "problem of a single story." Adichie (2009) uses this notion very eloquently to help us understand how prevalent stereotypes and assumptions are and how they shape learning and engagement. Both programs have drawn on her work to help students develop cultural competencies necessary for global citizenship.

International experiences might be another way to begin to consider such engagements. Experiences such as study abroad, however, are not always possible for the vast majority of U.S. college students, and only for a tiny minority, if any at all, of students located in institutions in the global South, no matter how wealthy or elite their institution may be. Programs therefore need to find creative ways of connecting across these divides. In the Global Studies major at Providence College, this recognition of the global ecology means intentionally connecting the local with the international. Each student in the program is required to study abroad, but also must take a one-credit Global Engagement course to prepare to study away, and then take a year-long Capstone course that includes an action research project in the local Providence community that often draws upon the students' experiences abroad. In the GCP at UCT, students use both local community knowledge to reflect on how global issues play out locally. Furthermore, there are rich opportunities in places such as UCT to engage the many foreign students who study at UCT as a way to bring the international to the local.

Technology is a powerful resource for the global ecology of education. As part of our growing collaboration, we were able to link students from a course of students returning from study abroad at Providence College (Crossing Borders) with a South African student involved with GCP. Our South African author was able to use interactive video technology to facilitate discussions among South African and American students when a Cape Town–based student recorded her own YouTube video drawing on the Adichie (2009) Ted Talk to critique accounts of her home, a township community on the outskirts of Cape Town, Khayelitsha (Ndzendze, 2014).

Conclusion: Challenges and Opportunities

Developing the capacity of leadership through a new lens will mean asking questions anew about higher education and its role in preparing future citizens as global leaders. It is not an easy task, however, and will take moral courage and vision. New kinds of leadership development are dependent on new ways of knowing, teaching, and learning, and being in the world—for both students and faculty alike. These are not easy changes: They require unlearning and reimagining practices, including power relationships both on campus and across the globe.

However, such new approaches also open up important opportunities for campuses, wherever they are located. New voices—of communities, of students, and of faculty, in different locations and differently positioned to more powerful global discourses—are provided with a space to be heard. These approaches also open up new possibilities for recognizing both curriculum and co-curriculum spaces—what Cowan (2010) calls "life-wide" learning opportunities—an integrating concept that can assimilate and connect learning in and from many different contexts (Jackson, 2010). This is important to explore for leadership learning going forward. Our hope is that both of our cases provide some insight into new approaches, frameworks, and experiences that can be drawn on for the future direction of education for global leadership: leadership practices through which students, communities, and faculty alike will grow and learn. In our rapidly globalizing and ever increasingly unequal world, this future can't come soon enough.

References

Adichie, C. (2009, July). The danger of a single story. *TedGlobal 2009*. Retrieved from http://www.ted.com/talks/chimamanda_adichie_the_danger_of_a_single_story

Alonso García, N., & Longo, N. (2015). Community voices: Integrating local and international partnerships through storytelling. *Partnerships: A Journal of Service-Learning and Civic Engagement, 6*(2), 1–18.

Astin, A. W., & Astin, H. S. (2000). *Leadership reconsidered: Engaging higher education in social change.* Retrieved from http://eric.ed.gov/?id=ED444437

Barber, B. (1998). Neither leaders nor followers: Citizenship under strong democracy. In B. Barber (Ed.), *A passion for democracy: American essays.* Princeton, NJ: Princeton University Press.

Beall, J., McMillan, J., & Small, J. (2010). *UCT Global Citizenship program: Curriculum framework document.* Cape Town, South Africa: University of Cape Town.

Boyle-Baise, M., Brown, R., Hsu, M.-C., Jones, D., Prakash, A., Rausch, M., & Wahlquist, Z. (2006). Learning service or service learning: Enabling the civic. *International Journal of Teaching and Learning in Higher Education, 18*(1), 17–26.

Boyte, H. (2014a, January 14). Beyond Mandela—South Africa's lessons for the world [Web log post]. Retrieved from http://www.huffingtonpost.com/harry-boyte/beyond-mandela-south-afri_b_4585581.html

Boyte, H. (2014b, February 10). Citizens at the centre of the globalizing world [Web log post]. Retrieved from http://sidnl.org/wordpress/wp-content/uploads/2014/02/Boyte-Civic-Politics-February-10.pdf

Cowan, J. (2010, April). Life-wide learning: "What matters to me as a teacher?" Paper presented at Enabling a More Complete Education: Encouraging, Recognizing and Valuing Life-Wide Learning in Higher Education Conference, University of Surrey, Guildford, Surrey, England. Retrieved from http://lifewidelearningconference.pbworks.com/w/page/24285296/E%20proceedings

Cremin, L. A. (1976). *Public education* (Vol. 1). New York, NY: Basic Books. Retrieved from http://www.tcrecord.org/library/abstract.asp?contentid=1184

Farmer, P. (2005). *Pathologies of power: Health, human rights, and the new war on the poor.* Berkeley, CA: University of California Press.

García, N. A., & Longo, N. V. (2013). Going global: Re-framing service-learning in an interconnected world. *Journal of Higher Education Outreach and Engagement, 17*(2), 111–135.

Gauteng, J., & Eastern Cape, P. (2013). *National youth engagement on national development plan 2013* [Data file]. Retrieved from http://www.inkulufreeheid.org/

Hart Research Associates. (1998). *New leadership for a new century: Key findings from a study on youth leadership and community service.* Washington, DC: Authors.

Hovey, R., Weinberg, A., & Bellamy, C. (2011). *Exploring leadership through international education: Civic learning through study abroad in Uganda* [Data file]. Retrieved from http://works.bepress.com/rebecca_hovey/10/

Jackson, N. (2010). *Enabling a more complete education.* In Lifewide learning Conference E-Proceedings version. Retrieved from http://lifewidelearningconference.pbworks.com/E-proceedings

Knight Abowitz, K., Raill-Jayanandhan, S., & Woiteshek, S. (2011). Public and community-based leadership education. In N. Longo & C. Gibson (Eds.), *From command to community: A new approach to leadership education in colleges and universities* (pp. 83–102). Medford, MA: Tufts University Press.

Leibowitz, B., Swartz, L. Bozalek, V., Carolissen, R., Nicholls, L., & Rohleder, P. (Eds.). (2012). *Community, self and identity: Educating South African university students for citizenship.* Cape Town, South Africa: Human Sciences Research Council.

Longo, N. V., & Gibson, C. M. (2011). *From command to community: A new approach to leadership education in colleges and universities.* Medford, MA: Tufts University Press. Retrieved from https://books.google.com/books?hl=en&lr=&id=sExEavrOxrQC&oi=fnd&pg=PP1&dq=Longo,+N.+and+Gibson.+C.+(Eds.)+(2011).+From+command+to+community:+a+new+approach+to+leadership+education+in+co

lleges+and+universities.+Medford,+MA:+Tufts+University+Press.&ots=f1jG1tGwPo&sig=gQGEKleRsKCYSRMNH_WJ2_mx7wE

Mangcu, X. (2012). African modernity and the struggle for people's power. *The Good Society, 21*(2), 279–299.

Mathews, D. (2009). Ships passing in the night? *Journal of Higher Education Outreach and Engagement, 13*(3), 5–16.

McMillan, J. (2013). *Teaching and learning for graduate attributes: UCT's Global Citizenship program* [data file]. Retrieved from www.socialresponsiveness.uct.ac.za/usr/social_resp/reports/SR_report_2013.pdf

McMillan, J., & Stanton, T. (2014). "Learning service" in international contexts: Partnership-based service-learning and research in Cape Town, South Africa. *Michigan Journal of Community Service Learning, 21*(1), 64–78.

Middleton, J. (2007). *Beyond authority: Leadership in a changing world.* New York, NY: Palgrave-MacMillan.

Mitchell, T., Visconti, V., Keene, A., & Battistoni, R. (2011). Educating for democratic leadership at Stanford, UMass, and Providence College. In N. V. Longo & C. M. Gibson (Eds.), *From command to community: A new approach to leadership education in colleges and universities* (pp. 115–148). Medford, MA: Tufts University Press.

Morphet, A. (1992). Introduction to the problems in adult learning. In B. Hutton (Ed.), *Adult basic education in South Africa: Literacy, English as a second language and numeracy* (pp. 87–102). Cape Town, South Africa: Oxford University Press.

Ndzendze, Z. (2014). *The concept of the single story.* Retrieved from https://www.youtube.com/watch?v=MNi2a-XQb1U&feature=youtu.be

Nussbaum, M. (2007). Cultivating humanity and world citizenship. *Future Forum.* Retrieved from http://chicagounbound.uchicago.edu/journal_articles/174/

Petriglieri, G. (2014, December 14). There is no shortage of leaders. *Harvard Business Review.* Retrieved from https://hbr.org/2014/12/there-is-no-shortage-of-leaders

Ransby, B. (2003). *Ella Baker and the Black freedom movement: A radical democratic vision.* Chapel Hill, NC: University of North Carolina Press. Retrieved from https://books.google.com/books?hl=en&lr=&id=DwGN3Z6ga28C&oi=fnd&pg=PR1&dq=+Ransby,+(2003).+Ella+Baker+and+the+black+freedom+movement&ots=qnWx0J1C1i&sig=i18EXPYy3oVaLLBghV6KshY1POU

Ross, C. (2011). *The leaderless revolution: How ordinary people will take power and change politics in the 21st century.* New York, NY: Blue Rider Press.

Simonelli, J., Earle, D., & Story, E. (2004). Acompanar obediciendo: Learning to help in collaboration with Zapatista communities. *Michigan Journal of Community Service Learning, 10*(3), 43–56.

Soudien, C. (2006). The city, citizenship, and education. *Journal of Education, 40,* 103–116.

NICHOLAS V. LONGO *is chair and professor in Global Studies at Providence College.*

JANICE MCMILLAN *is a senior lecturer at the University of Cape Town.*

NEW DIRECTIONS FOR STUDENT LEADERSHIP • DOI: 10.1002/yd

This chapter details the ways youth community organizing strategies can inform leadership educators' approaches to engaging marginalized youth in leadership development for social change.

International Perspectives on Youth Leadership Development Through Community Organizing

Rashida H. Govan, Jesica Siham Fernandez, Deana G. Lewis, Ben Kirshner

Over the past 10 years, interest in community organizing has risen significantly, due in part to the influence of President Barack Obama (Shirley, 2009). Although this attention may be recent, community organizing efforts of marginalized youth have historically spurred many of the world's major social movements (Ginwright, Noguera, & Cammarota, 2006). Globally the collective wisdom and action of youth in the anti-Apartheid movement, the Civil Rights movement, and more recently, the Arab Spring and the #Blacklivesmatter movements, have brought about significant social change.

Marginalized youth are defined in this chapter as youth who are inequitably and negatively impacted by societal, systemic, and institutional barriers. These youth face mounting challenges, including limited access to quality education, the school-to-prison pipeline, unemployment, and poverty. It is important that leadership educators identify effective strategies to build the leadership capacity of youth to enact positive social change. An examination of international youth community organizing (YCO) groups illuminates pathways to leadership for marginalized youth and offers strategies for K–16 institutions to build youth capacity effectively to serve as change agents.

This chapter explores key practices of community organizing groups that facilitate youth leadership development. We draw on examples from a subset of data within an international study on youth community organizing that examines the learning experiences of marginalized youth engaged

NEW DIRECTIONS FOR STUDENT LEADERSHIP, no. 148, Winter 2015 © 2015 Wiley Periodicals, Inc., A Wiley Company
Published online in Wiley Online Library (wileyonlinelibrary.com) • DOI: 10.1002/yd.20155

in organizing across seven different organizations on three different conti-
nents. We identify four practices that are critical for the leadership development of young people: prioritizing youth voice, positive relationships,
critical social analysis, and active engagement.

Leadership Development Within Youth Community Organizing

In YCO settings, youth development and grassroots organizing strategies
are applied to build youth's capacity to become activists and change agents
in their own lives and communities (Delgado & Staples, 2008; Ginwright
et al., 2006; Watts, Griffith, & Abdul-Adil, 1999). Youth are viewed as citizens who have a right to be engaged in the resistance, deconstruction, and
reformation of institutionalized systems of oppression (Ginwright, 2001).
Not only do youth have the right to resist and reform systems of oppression, but youth are also viewed as being well positioned to identify and deconstruct social problems, and develop strategies to remedy them (Torre &
Fine, 2006). Thus, leadership development practices within YCO settings
focus on the development of youth's sociopolitical awareness of institutionalized oppression and on acquiring the skills to engage in community organizing activities toward social justice (Delgado & Staples, 2008; Ginwright
et al., 2006).

Study Background.   Examples presented in this chapter are drawn
from an international study of community-based youth organizing. The
study, led by Dr. Roderick Watts, examined young people's learning and
development from seven organizations: four in the United States, one in
Ireland, one in Northern Ireland, and one in South Africa. Each of the organizations involved in the study is situated in urban settings, although the
areas that some of the organizations served extended beyond the borders of
these major metropolitan areas.

The four research sites in the United States work directly with marginalized youth in urban settings. The Kenwood Oakland Community Organization (KOCO) in Chicago, IL, works primarily with low-income, working-
class African American youth and families, and is regarded as a multigenerational, multi-issue organization that provides social services and community organizing. Youth work at KOCO focuses on training and developing
youth leaders by actively involving them in campaigns, meetings, and organizing work that centers on equitable education, affordable housing, youth
investment, and senior living. KOCO is best known for its call for an investigation into civil rights violations at Dyett High School, which led to the
launch of a three-city investigation.

Padres & Jovenes Unidos (Padres), located in Denver, CO, is a multigenerational, multiracial, member-led organization that is committed to organizing efforts on racial justice, immigrant rights, health justice, civic engagement, and educational excellence for all people. Specific campaign issues addressed by youth include ending the school-to-prison pipeline, civic

engagement, and immigrant student rights. The organization's youth-led Campaign to End the School-to-Jail track was one of the country's first and has won local and statewide victories that have led the field and garnered national attention.

In New Orleans, the Vietnamese American Young Leaders Association (VAYLA) is regarded as a progressive, youth-led, multi-issue, multiracial, community-based organization whose organizing efforts have focused on educational justice, language access, and environmental justice. The organization provides youth with tools, skills, and resources to build political power. The organization also provides support services for youth and their families and has garnered national attention for its educational advocacy in post-Katrina New Orleans.

The final U.S. site, Coleman Advocates for Children and Youth (Coleman), is in San Francisco, and is identified as a multiracial, member-led community organization characterized by a bottom-up approach toward social change. Coleman links community activism with policy advocacy and leadership development. Youth organizing efforts focus on education justice, economic justice, and broad civic engagement. The organization has gained national recognition for much of its work, including recent work to end the school-to-prison pipeline.

In South Africa, the Cape Town-based organization Equal Education (EE) works on national issues and has active membership in multiple provinces in South Africa. EE focuses on changing systemic inequities in the education system. The most active participants in this multigenerational organization are the high school members who engage heavily in organizing work. The organization currently focuses on establishing minimum norms and standards for schools, such that they provide resources and infrastructure across the country.

In Belfast, Northern Ireland, and Dublin, Ireland, the context for YCO is quite different. Neither of these groups describes itself as organizing groups in the same way that we use this term in a U.S. or South African context. Instead, their primary aim was youth civic learning and engagement (in Belfast) or youth wellness and holistic development (in Dublin). Where is My Public Servant (WIMPS), the program in Belfast, uses new media to foster communication and accountability between youth and policymakers and is a program of an international model of civic engagement called Public Achievement. Young people work in teams to identify public problems, study them, and raise awareness or take action using media tools and participation in policy settings. Youth are organized in chapters that draw young people from both Protestant and Catholic communities in Belfast neighborhoods and other cities in Northern Ireland.

In Dublin, the participating organization is called The FamiliBase, a multiservice youth center located in a working class suburb. The FamiliBase offers a range of programs and services to young people, including support groups for young mothers and fathers, opportunities to perform and record music, and support for mental health and wellness. The center places emphasis on youth voice and leadership, and has created multiple opportunities for youth to form groups to work on community issues or participate in political forums. Despite the different local context and terminology, we sought to include Belfast and Dublin groups in the study because they shared with the other groups an emphasis on youth leadership and voice. We believe that audiences focused on student leadership in North America can learn a great deal from this cross-national study, while acknowledging the important differences.

The purpose of the study was to identify civic engagement and youth development outcomes associated with YCO and the kinds of learning ecologies that fostered those outcomes. The primary mode of data collection was ethnography carried out by local researchers over a 18–24 month span, including observations, meetings, interviews, and artifact analysis. These qualitative data were supplemented with surveys administered at two time points. For this chapter we draw primarily on field notes; we supplement these field notes with some examples from interviews with youth organizers.

Leadership Development in YCO Settings.   We identified four distinctive aspects of leadership development in YCO settings that help cultivate the personal power of marginalized youth. These features build the capacity of youth to understand and dismantle systems of oppression in order to enact change in their lives and further the aim of social justice.

Prioritizing Youth Voice.   Most of the youth engaged in our study share the common experience of having a marginalized identity or belonging to a marginalized community. Youth have limited opportunities to speak as authorities on issues of oppression. Within YCO settings, youth are regarded as experts and their voices and perspectives are prioritized.

YCO provides a platform for youth to amplify their voices on critical issues in their communities and serve as a meeting place for youth with shared experiences to build solidarity. The international study on YCO offers myriad examples of youth engaged as authorities on issues in their schools and communities, and as drivers of the agendas of these organizations. For instance, in one meeting in San Francisco, a youth organizer asked peers if they ever felt oppressed by a teacher or an adult in their schools. The conversation that unfolded unveiled experiences with double standards in enforcement of dress codes and the negative interpretation of the behavior of Black and Latino youth in schools:

> ... In schools some girls get in trouble for dressing in certain ways, and guys get in trouble for the type of clothes they wear and the colors (red or blue). And that if they look Latino or Black they get in worse trouble because teachers think that they are up to no good.

NEW DIRECTIONS FOR STUDENT LEADERSHIP • DOI: 10.1002/yd

Another youth in Denver shared:

> ... In Padres, right now we're being taught how to speak truth to power and how to stand up for yourself and for others. And in school, I guess it would be probably hard because at the same time, your whole life, you've been taught that you have to listen to your elders. Taught to respect them and that you can't speak to them like—the truth—to them if you're being taught that they're the ones who are always right and you're just a speck of a thing that they don't care about.

Youth within the study frequently referenced the experience of being silenced and feeling devalued within schools, religious institutions, and homes. YCO settings are regarded as distinctly different because youth have freedom to speak for themselves. This experience of autonomy within YCO settings emboldens youth. The following excerpt from a young person at the New Orleans site highlights this experience:

> VAYLA is simply, it's just a beautiful place ... it's beautiful in the way it's run. I've never ever been in a place where there are so many students passionate about the same thing. I've never been in a place where what students said counted. I've never been in a place where they actually have resources to make other people see that student voice counts. I've never been in a position where I feel like I can make changes. And I've never been in a place where I can see myself grow.

An organizer at Equal Education echoed this sentiment, saying,

> This organization was so different from any organization I've been to. Like, education is important. I wanted to be part of this organization; there is no other organization that is working with the youth and encouraging the youth to stand on their own to do something with their schools.

Thus, YCO settings offer opportunities for youth to examine their experiences with marginalization while maintaining an organizational culture that encourages youth to use their voices and their experiences to enact change.

Positive Relationships. Relationships are critical to community organizing work and are also pivotal to the leadership development of youth in YCO. The organizations in the study described their approach to age and power in slightly different ways: as either intergenerational, youth–adult partnerships, or youth-centered. Intergenerational signals that people of all ages and generations participate—and that the organization gains more insight and power when parents and young people are organizing together. Youth–adult partnerships, closely related to intergenerational, describe the collaborative relationships in which both adult and youth voices are privileged/valued in decision making. Youth-centered pertains to relationships where youth and adults are viewed equally, and an organization's work and agenda are youth-directed and driven. Although these characteristics are aspirational, each organization in our study is structured in a way that intentionally values youth voice and engages youth in decision making within the organization (e.g., youth hold formal positions and are involved in consensus-building decision-making processes).

Our observation and interview data indicate that the supportive relationship between youth and adults bolsters youth efficacy, agency, and commitment to YCO. Adults within YCO settings build strong, mutually supportive relationships with youth and advocate for their leadership roles. In some instances, adults play the role of an adult supporter (i.e., adult allies who serve as a resource to youth in facilitating the youth's agenda and in supporting youth development, especially of agency). Similarly, peer relationships operate in much the same way, creating a sense of belonging that facilitates youth commitment to the organizations in which they are developing their leadership capacity. Positive relationships also serve as an important source of social support for youth, which in turn facilitates and reinforces youth's leadership development and commitment to YCO.

At Coleman, we observed a meeting where one of the youth organizers recounted tragedy in his life. This example illustrates how positive relationships between staff people and youth helped build community, trust, and encouragement:

> Cesar began to read his crumpled up piece of folded paper. As he rapped about his life, he mentioned the death of his younger brother and what that loss was like for him. He talked about his feelings and emotions, and how he promised to make each day count and make each moment worth it, because he has a chance and his little brother didn't. There was a lot of emotion; several people in tears as they listened to Cesar's deep voice shatter a bit as he fought to keep his tears inside. Toya asked Cesar if he wanted to continue and Cesar said that he didn't know he was going to feel that way. Paul said that he really appreciated Cesar putting himself out there and talking so deeply about his emotions, and he added, "It takes courage."

In this excerpt, Cesar's willingness to be vulnerable illustrates a process we observed at multiple sites. Deep and intentional relationships, focused on healing and solidarity, engender trust, a sense of family, and commitment to transforming systems of oppression.

In another excerpt from the Dublin site, one youth described her perceptions of the organization:

> We've grown into a whole little family that it's amazing that we hang around with each other outside, inside and go away together, go on holidays together

that we pay for, go on exchanges that FamiliBase pays for … we're so close, that's how close we are.

At WIMPS, one of the participants contrasted her power relative to adults within the YCO with the lack of power and choice she experienced at her school.

(It's) very stressful to learn something that you don't really want to learn. It's not gonna happen, and then you get—you literally get shouted at for not learning it, when you can't learn it. Because if you don't want to learn it, you're not gonna listen to it. You're not gonna take it in. With WIMPS it's literally, what do you want to do? How do you want to do it, and when do you want to have it done by? It really is what you want, and it's really what your voice wants to say. I think that's a big difference, is that it really is free reign here.

In this example the importance of youth as decision makers within YCO settings and the emancipatory value of this experience, as opposed to the more hierarchical relationships in school settings, is highlighted. The more collaborative or horizontal power structures of YCO groups positively impact youth–adult relationships and prepare youth to be colleagues with adults. Relationships within YCO groups also focus on healing from experiences with oppression. The focus on youth well-being is important to promoting youth leaders' commitment to leadership activities focused on transforming communities and institutions. The positive relationships described above bring these youth from the margins to the center of YCO, a seemingly rare experience for marginalized youth.

Critical Social Analysis. YCO groups served as settings where marginalized youth created transformative spaces to engage in critical social analysis (CSA). We define CSA as a process of sharing and reflecting through facilitated dialogues, and forms of narrative and visual expression, which link people's experiences to social structures and systematic forms of power and oppression. All of the participating organizations placed central importance on helping young people develop a critical lens that facilitates and reinforces their sociopolitical development as leaders and change agents.

This process of dialogue and reflection is shown in field notes taken at Coleman:

Lina stands up to write on the white board and Erika asks us all to share the words that come to our mind when we think about power. Several of the youth share out loud some of the words that come to their minds, among these are: "money, force of energy, corruption, dictators, media, people, dirty politicians, white supremacy, manipulation, influence over decision making, 1%, capitalism, control over circumstances." Erika then asked youth a follow up question: "How do people use their power to oppress other people? How do you see people using their power?" Among some of the responses given by youth were: "to destroy other people, to control, to keep their power, for greater control of the people, to distribute power, to empower people, to get things for themselves and that work in their favor, for a better life, and to oppress other people." Erika then mentioned, "There are two types of power: 1) institutional power and 2) people power."

In these facilitated dialogues, youth named how systems of power, and power holders, shape their lives and the lives of their communities, that is, how structures, such as capitalism and White supremacy, operate to oppress other people. This practice of categorizing their experiences within oppressive social structures demonstrated their awareness of the relationships between their lived experiences and the systems of power that impact them. (See Chapter 1 for similar strategies for raising power consciousness as a leadership education tool.)

Youth participated in a follow-up activity that used concepts and terms they generated earlier to create a visual representation of institutional power.

Crystal was assigned to be the writer/drawer, and so she drew an image of the White House to represent the place where decisions that affect other institutions in society get made. Manuel mentioned that the drawing of the White House looked like Capitol Hill. The next image that Crystal drew was a school, and this was based on Jackie's suggestion, who mentioned that schools were also an institution that received money from the government, and that the government determined what schools should do for some states. Paul asked if that related to Khalil's comment about prisons. Crystal said that it did and she suggested drawing the school behind some prison bars.

The revolutionary language youth collectively produced was further represented in their discussion of the drawings and symbols they used to illustrate examples of institutional power in their lives. The connections youth made to unequal distribution of power, quality education, and prisons were similar to those made by youth at other YCO sites. For example, youth leaders at Equal Education, called *equalizers*, were asked to reflect on what they had learned in the last term about inequality. One of the equalizers spoke about the teach-in at UCT and how she learned that inequality was caused by capitalists that control big businesses and do not pay workers enough money to help their families survive. At Coleman and Equal Education young people reflected upon the ways in which power influenced their lives. Youth also collectively examined issues of systemic oppression. This process of collectively sharing and reflecting directed their CSA away from self-blame and toward a more structural understanding, which allowed them to deconstruct their oppressive social conditions within various contexts.

Schools, for example, are one specific setting where youth often experienced institutionalized oppression. Researchers discussed with students their impressions of school settings. Students mentioned several restrictions, among these: (1) not being able to use phones; (2) having to come in through back doors, which one student compared to "slavery times"; (3) excessive building use restrictions, thereby creating a "prison like environment" according to another student; (4) zero-tolerance policies enacted by teachers; and (5) school uniform policies. In the course of generating their list, youth drew parallels between schools and prisons, and made salient the school-to-prison pipeline. CSA emerged out of these and other forms of systemic oppression, as well as the conditions or processes through which youth were able to share, reflect, and discuss social problems beyond individual stories, and as histories of community/collective struggle. CSA is particularly important in facilitating youth agency and leadership, because it is focused on dismantling systems of oppression and catalyzing youth's collective power to enact social change.

Active Engagement.   The groups we studied organized their schedules and work cycles around campaigns to build political power and hold public officials accountable to their constituents. These campaigns provided extended opportunities to learn leadership by doing leadership. Across the five sites we observed a range of opportunities for youth to enact leadership, including participation on hiring committees, recruiting peers to school chapters of the YCO groups, engaging in public speech to elected officials, facilitating workshops for peers, handling logistics for youth summits, and strategic planning discussions about messaging and publicity. The young people enacting these roles were those directly affected by the issues at hand. A young person who had been suspended several times from school, for example, would be the person educating the school board about the school-to-prison pipeline, or a young person in South Africa who had been wrongfully treated by her principal would be organizing her school chapter. In our analysis of these opportunities for action, three themes of leadership development stand out.

Accelerated Learning.   We did not see an extended waiting period before newcomers began to step into new roles. On the contrary, it appeared that if you showed up and an important event was on the horizon, there would be a role for you to play. Often this role involved stepping onto a public stage to speak. Less experienced youth might rely on scaffolding, such as a script or note cards, to support their first time speaking in public. For example, at the Denver site, there were numerous times during an accountability meeting with the school district where young people spoke up. Each time they introduced themselves using the same general pattern: "My name is _____, I'm in (grade in school), and I'm pre-college ... not pre-prison!" This structured quality, we believe, made it more accessible for a novice speaker to participate. Sometimes, however, speaking engagements were far less scripted and called for improvisation. We saw this in Denver too, where youth became skilled at holding their own in interactions with public officials. Or consider this recollection from a youth organizer from Coleman:

> At Coleman you get a lot of like, "Hey, we're going to the meeting, you're facilitating and you got to talk to like 30 people ..." So you got to learn how to improv ... Like cuz you are put in a lot of different situations, "Okay, we have to be here in 12 minutes and you need to know this whole pack of information." You'll be like, "Oh man." You just learn to move kind of high paced.

Accounts of public speaking scenarios like this showed up a great deal in our data, particularly interviews, suggesting that they were a rich source of leadership learning for youth. Youth talked about overcoming nervousness or feelings of intimidation by remembering their strategic goals and relying on peers for support.

Planning and Decision Making.   All five of the groups encouraged strong cultures of consultation with youth and/or joint planning. For the organization in South Africa, which supported multiple youth groups distributed across cities and provinces of South Africa, it was particularly important to create systems for bidirectional decision making, in order to build a social movement of which all felt ownership. For this reason Equal Education organized regular mass meetings where young people from across regions would come together to discuss plans and strategy. The following example is drawn from a mass meeting where different youth groups convened to discuss suggestions for how to publicize the upcoming deadline for the government to report back on its progress implementing the national "Norms and Standards" agreement for school infrastructure:

> Tshepiso then went up to the podium and requested that the comrades sit down for proceedings to continue. When people had settled down Tshepiso then asked scribes from each group to come to the front and present the suggestions that their respective groups submitted ... After the last suggestion had been made, one of the staff people took to the podium to point that, "we are going to draft a plan based on these suggestions tomorrow when we meet for a secretariat meeting. We will then circulate the draft to some people who are normally accessible to us for feedback.

This culture of shared planning generated multiple creative ideas for strategic communications. These included giving out information at the "taxi ranks" (transportation hubs for people commuting to work from the townships), burial societies, and churches.

Debrief and Reflection.   A third core element of active engagement was what happened after, in terms of debrief and reflection. Group reflection was a regular feature of the action cycle in most of the organizations. These debriefs were often facilitated by a young adult staff person who acted as coach or mentor to the youth leaders. The following is a typical example:

> Kris (adult) asked if there were any other thoughts or impressions from that day, and Francisco added that he felt good that he was able to go up there and talk; he added that he felt good about himself, "I had a part in this too." Roxanna added that even though she had spoken at other events, she still felt nervous to talk in front of "old white people." Karen asked her what made her nervous, and Roxanna said that she knew that they had a lot of power, and it was hard for her to keep calm and communicate effectively about something she cared about and was affected by. Kris added that all of the youth who showed up were powerful speakers.

In other examples we observed discussions about whether the group had achieved its goals and where they had fallen short. Staff members at Padres were particularly mindful of how people in positions of power wielded their influence not only through intimidation or hostility, but also by making friendly overtures or giving out cell phone information to youth. Staff there provided feedback or coaching about how to hold people accountable even when the political figure was friendly or claimed good intentions.

Recommendations for Youth Leadership Development in K–16 Settings

YCO groups provide young people with resources and tools to facilitate their leadership development and support social action. The social actions youth undertake result from a critical awareness that social conditions must be changed via collective forms of engagement with communities and institutions. YCO deconstructs disempowering discourses about youth from racially, economically, and politically marginalized communities. In the place of these common, yet damaging narratives, youth, and their communities, produce counterhegemonic narratives of young people and their development.

YCOs incorporate youth voice in decision making and regard youth perspectives as paramount to the work of these organizations. These organizational characteristics are essential to youth leadership development because they help facilitate a sense of agency in youth. Because they are regarded as experts in their own lives, youth are encouraged to participate in critical social analysis and problem-solving opportunities in which they develop the skills to address social issues affecting them and their communities. Education institutions can benefit from examining the organizational culture of YCOs to identify areas where youth are regarded as experts, and where youth have opportunities to use that expertise to influence decision making. Through such an examination, education institutions can also identify areas where these opportunities can be created and institutionalized to foster youth leadership development.

Prioritizing youth voice also requires centering youth experiences. Educational institutions can examine the ways in which youth experiences with oppression are addressed in schools, especially in classroom learning. How are classroom lessons, or the material being taught in schools, preparing youth to solve social issues they face in their communities directly? Incorporating their lived experiences into classroom learning provides youth with an advantage in addressing classroom assignments and helps them see themselves as change agents, a critical step in developing agency in leadership development.

A focus on positive relationships in K–12 educational institutions is sometimes deprioritized because of the heavy emphasis on standardized testing and the achievement orientation of these systems. YCO settings place great currency on relationships and establish collaborative or horizontal power structures. These organizational structures encourage accountability and leadership in youth by seeking their perspectives in the creation of agendas, strategies, and advocacy.

Furthermore, YCO settings are hubs of healing from oppression. The organizations in our study recognize the important role that positive and supportive relationships play in promoting healing among youth who have experienced oppression. Healing is a key step in building solidarity toward enacting social change, and YCOs help build relationships that affirm and help combat what we call "oppression fatigue": the weariness from experiences with social oppression that diminishes one's emotional well-being and energy to resist social oppression. Educational settings can mimic this dynamic to forge working relationships between youth and adults to foster their leadership development.

We recommend that youth leadership programs emphasize opportunities for direct interaction between students and institutional decision makers or education policy makers. Opportunities for direct contact between students and decision makers are rare; too often they are limited solely to expressive politics or presentations without opportunity for dialogue and debate. Young people benefit from chances to prepare for such encounters, including role plays, where they practice responding to hostile or patronizing responses from adults and other power holders.

YCO settings develop the leadership capacity of youth by soliciting their perspectives and insights on key issues and decisions, by cultivating positive relationships characterized by shared power and empathy, by developing youth's critical social analysis, and through active engagement in social change efforts. Two key themes present in this analysis of these settings are power and liberation, both of which represent core aims of leadership, particularly for marginalized people. These themes were embedded in the objectives of the leadership development activities we observed.

YCO organizations help youth discover their personal and collective power, as well as strategies toward building their power in solidarity with other youth and adults. These practices cultivated a way for youth to institutionalize their power and presence within YCO settings. Thus, the greatest lesson on leadership development that can be gleaned from YCO settings is that organizations concerned with this realm of development must both reflect and pursue the aim of power and liberation for all.

References

Delgado, M., & Staples, L. (2008). *Youth-led community organizing: Theory and action.* New York, NY: Oxford University Press.

Ginwright, S. (2001). Critical resistance: African American youth and US racism. *Youth Development Journal, 3,* 15–24.

Ginwright, S., Noguera, P., & Cammarota, J. (Eds.). (2006). *Beyond resistance: Youth activism and community change.* New York, NY: Routledge.

Shirley, D. (2009). Community organizing and educational change: A reconnaissance. *Journal of Educational Change, 10,* 229–237.

Torre, M. E., & Fine, M. (2006). Participatory action research (PAR) by youth. In L. Sherrod (Ed.), *Youth activism: An international encyclopedia* (pp. 456–462). Westport, CT: Greenwood.

Watts, R. J., Griffith, D. M., & Abdul-Adil, J. (1999). Sociopolitical development as an antidote for oppression-theory and action. *American Journal of Community Psychology, 27*(2), 255–271.

Rashida Govan is the project director for the International Study on Youth Community Organizing and earned her Ph.D. from the University of New Orleans in educational leadership and administration.

Jesica Siham Fernandez is an adjunct faculty in the ethnic studies program at Santa Clara University, and member of the Research Justice at the Intersections (RJI) scholars program affiliated with the Ethnic Studies Department at Mills College.

Deana G. Lewis is a doctoral student in educational policy studies with a concentration in gender and women's studies at the University of Illinois at Chicago.

Ben Kirshner is an associate professor of education at the University of Colorado Boulder and faculty director of CU Engage: Center for Community-Based Learning and Research.

Index

NEW DIRECTIONS FOR STUDENT LEADERSHIP

ORDER FORM SUBSCRIPTION AND SINGLE ISSUES

DISCOUNTED BACK ISSUES:

Use this form to receive 20% off all back issues of *New Directions for Student Leadership*.
All single issues priced at **$23.20** (normally $29.00)

TITLE   ISSUE NO.   ISBN

_____   _____   _____

_____   _____   _____

_____   _____   _____

*Call 1-800-835-6770 or see mailing instructions below. When calling, mention the promotional code JBNND to receive
your discount. For a complete list of issues, please visit www.wiley.com/WileyCDA/WileyTitle/productCd-YD.html*

SUBSCRIPTIONS: (1 YEAR, 4 ISSUES)

☐ New Order   ☐ Renewal

U.S.	☐ Individual: $89	☐ Institutional: $363
CANADA/MEXICO	☐ Individual: $89	☐ Institutional: $405
ALL OTHERS	☐ Individual: $113	☐ Institutional: $441

*Call 1-800-835-6770 or see mailing and pricing instructions below.
Online subscriptions are available at www.onlinelibrary.wiley.com*

ORDER TOTALS:

Issue / Subscription Amount: $ _____

Shipping Amount: $ _____
(for single issues only – subscription prices include shipping)

Total Amount: $ _____

SHIPPING CHARGES:

First Item $6.00
Each Add'l Item $2.00

*(No sales tax for U.S. subscriptions. Canadian residents, add GST for subscription orders. Individual rate subscriptions must
be paid by personal check or credit card. Individual rate subscriptions may not be resold as library copies.)*

BILLING & SHIPPING INFORMATION:

☐ **PAYMENT ENCLOSED:** *(U.S. check or money order only. All payments must be in U.S. dollars.)*

☐ **CREDIT CARD:**   ☐ VISA   ☐ MC   ☐ AMEX

Card number _____Exp. Date_____

Card Holder Name_____Card Issue # _____

Signature _____Day Phone_____

☐ **BILL ME:** *(U.S. institutional orders only. Purchase order required.)*

Purchase order # _____
           Federal Tax ID 13559302 • GST 89102-8052

Name_____

Address_____

Phone_____ E-mail_____

Copy or detach page and send to: **John Wiley & Sons, Inc. / Jossey Bass**
                                      PO Box 55381
                                      Boston, MA 02205-9850

PROMO JBNND

CPSIA information can be obtained
at www.ICGtesting.com
Printed in the USA
LVHW021716210319
611422LV00021B/1120/P